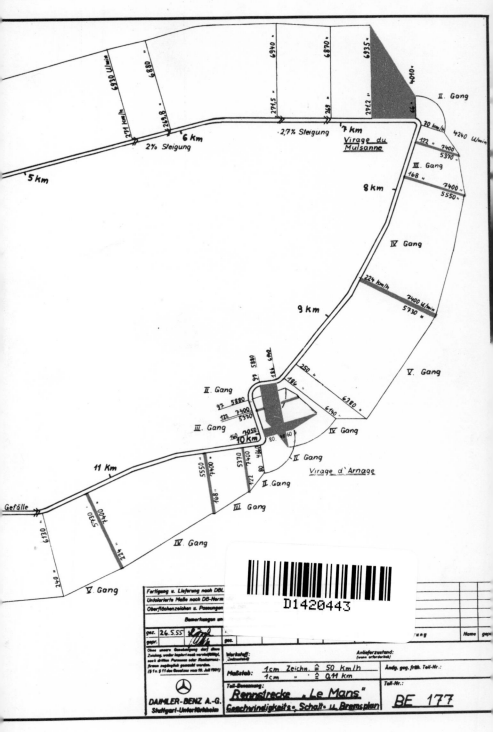

Code X15

D1420443

Fertigung u. Lieferung nach DBL
Untolerierte Maße nach DB-Norm
Oberflächenzeichen u. Passungen

Bemerkungen un

gez. 26.5.55
gepr.

Ohne unsere Genehmigung darf dieser
Zeichng. weder kopiert noch vervielfältigt,
noch dritten Personen oder Nachbaren-
firmen zugänglich gemacht werden.
(§ 1 u. § 11 des Gesetzes vom 19. Juli 1901)

Werkstoff:
Jedenstahl

Maßstab: 1cm Zeichn. ≙ 50 Km/h
            1cm   "   ≙ 0,11 km

Antieferzustand:
(wenn erforderlich)

Ändg. geg. früh. Teil-Nr.:

Teil-Benennung: Rennstrecke „Le Mans"
Geschwindigkeits-, Schalt- u. Bremsplan

Teil-Nr.: BE 177

DAIMLER-BENZ A.-G.
Stuttgart-Untertürkheim

Name gep

DEATH RACE – LE MANS 1955

By the same author

A Handbook of Motor Racing and Rallying, 1970
Mexico or Bust: the World Cup Rally
The Day I Died

Mark Kahn

Death Race
Le Mans 1955

BARRIE & JENKINS
COMMUNICA · EUROPA

First published in 1976 by
Barrie & Jenkins Limited
24 Highbury Crescent, London N5 1RX

Copyright © Mark Kahn, 1976

ISBN 0 214 20284 4

Printed in Great Britain by The Anchor Press Ltd
and bound by Wm Brendon & Son Ltd
both of Tiptree, Essex

CONTENTS

Introduction

Why rake it all up now after more than twenty years? The question was asked of me more than once in my research, and I found it disconcerting, not because I was at a loss for an answer, but because I had assumed that it was self-evident. But, thinking about it, I feel that the question does demand an overt answer. It may be helpful and perhaps interest the reader if I recount how the book came into being.

I had no intention of writing about the Le Mans disaster. I had written a book dealing with crashes involving some famous racing drivers – all of whom had survived against every probability. It was while the book was being serialised by the *Sunday Mirror* that my office phone there rang, and a voice said: 'You don't know me. My name is Macklin . . .' Macklin. I knew the name. Of course I knew it. 'Are you,' I asked, '*Lance* Macklin?' The owner of the voice agreed that that was indeed his name. 'Good God,' I said, 'we've never met, but I've seen you race often . . . years ago.' It was not perhaps the most tactful of remarks, but Mr Macklin was not offended. He said: 'I have been reading your articles. You know, I was one of the central figures in the Le Mans disaster, and my story has never been told.'

Now no journalist can hear the words 'story has never been told' without feeling a stirring of the blood and an irresistible compulsion to know more – however often it may have transpired that what has not been told is not worth the telling. I met Mr Macklin and found what he had to say very well worth telling. I was fascinated, not merely because of my feeling for motor racing, but with the story in its own right. As history.

7

It was too late to incorporate it into my book, or the *Sunday Mirror* articles extracted from it, but in any case this would have been inadequate. Others have written about the Le Mans disaster, but in isolated and somewhat scrappy single chapters, rather like hostesses leading guests hurriedly past a shabby room. The more I delved, the more convinced I became that Macklin's story ought to be told, and indeed the whole story of that tragic 24-hour race, and that it needed not a chapter, but a book. Moreover, it appears to me, those writers who have dealt with that Le Mans have been partisan, deeply concerned to defend Mike Hawthorn.

Mr 'Lofty' England, Jaguar's racing team manager at the time, and later the firm's chairman, gave me his view: 'The inquiry into what happened was responsibly conducted, and for anybody to start apportioning blame now is wrong.'

It is not my object, nor Mr Macklin's – although in his view the inquiry was a farce – to apportion blame. What I have done is to try to show *what happened* through the eyes of some of those who were there. It is true, as Mr England points out, that several witnesses to, say, the same road accident will give as many different versions of events, each in the honest belief that his is the 'correct' one. But the reader will have to form conclusions – if that is what he wants to do – in the awareness of precisely this trap. At all events, it seems to me that one ought not to shirk recording history because one's sources are human and fallible. It would be an impossible world for historians of all sorts if that consideration deterred them.

I am well aware that some people may disapprove for reasons unconcerned with the accuracy of the book. Mr Eoin Young, the well-known motor-sport journalist, wrote in *Autocar* of an encounter we had at Dijon, where I had gone to interview Fangio: 'Mark Kahn is a Fleet Street journalist who has an interest in motor sport. Kahn has done several major rallies and written books on the subject. He also wrote a book, *The Day I Died*, that may not have been to the purist's taste, but which dealt with several top drivers talking about their most monumental crash. . . .'

Who are the purists? What are they that reality doth offend them? I imagine that those to whom Mr Young was referring are people who feel that it is not quite nice, more, that it is even caddish, for anyone to draw attention to things that ought to be left in decent obscurity. Only an outsider would be so indelicate as to bring into the open such vulgar and disturbing matters as violent death, terror, misjudgment, confusion, and even dramatic tension. But why are such people called purists? What on earth has obscurantism to do with purity? Dear ostriches, life itself is far from 'pure' in your terms. I blush for it, but there it undoubtedly is.

The Le Mans disaster is part of history. I suppose it would be possible to write of Tudor England, say, without mentioning the Court of Star Chamber, the burnings of Mary, the cruelties and the squalor as well as the triumphs and the achievements. But it wouldn't be history. And it seemed to me that one ought to contribute to this history while there are still people who can say, 'Yes, I was there. I actually saw . . .'

I do not make the claim that this book is an academic history, if such a thing were possible. It is a documentary. But history, of a sort, none the less. In writing it I have portrayed the lives of the three principal actors as germane to the issue. And through them, I have attempted to present a picture of the sort of world they lived in, as a distinct era, the romantic era, of motor sport and its social background. I believe that somehow the Le Mans disaster marked the end of the era. Or at any rate, the beginning of the end.

I wish to express my gratitude to those who talked freely to me and gave so generously of their time especially as some had serious misgivings about the purpose for which I was talking to them. I do not include them among the aforementioned ostriches. In particular I am grateful to Mr England who helped so greatly despite his disapproval. And also to Mr Andrew Whyte, of Jaguar, who gave unstinted assistance against his own misgivings. I would like to record, not merely my thanks, but my respect for their viewpoint, although I do not share it, and can only hope that the result will not be too distasteful to them. I must express, too, my gratitude to Mercedes-Benz for their kindness to me at Stuttgart where I was given every facility. The archives were opened for me and documents made available, as was the unique Uhlenhaut diagram of the circuit, showing speeds and gear changes, which figures in the book. My thanks are also due to Mr Derek Tye of the RAC for

9

some invaluable research, and to Mr Peter Jopp, my companion on several international rallies, who not only figures in the book, but read the typescript to ensure its accuracy, and who answered my queries with a patience and good humour exceeding that which he showed when we were driving together to Monte Carlo or Mexico. Thanks are due also to William Kimber for permission to quote from Mike Hawthorn's book *Challenge Me the Race* and to Gentry Books for permission to quote from *The Day I Died*.

Above all, thanks to Lance Macklin for a telephone call he made to me which began . . . 'You don't know me. My name is Macklin . . .'

Warm-up laps

A lone car came out of the Arnage hairpin bend on a classic-
ally correct line. It's colour: British racing green. As he
accelerated away, the driver, Lance Macklin, glanced in his
mirror, then turned his head for a better look. A whole group
of cars was going into the corner. They were the leaders of the
Le Mans 24-Hour Endurance Race. It had been going on for
almost two and a half hours, and Macklin knew that soon,
very soon, he was going to be lapped. For the second time.

It didn't particularly bother him. He was experienced and
able – the adjective brilliant was habitually applied to him
when his name appeared in the newspapers. This was his sixth
Le Mans. He knew and had to accept that his Austin-Healey
with its 2662 cc engine, virtually a production car, couldn't
compete for an outright win with the big boys, the Ferraris,
the D-type Jaguars, the Mercedes, intensively developed and
prepared and, unlike the Austin-Healey, bearing little relation
to a motor car that anyone could buy and run on the road. But
an outright win, although the most glittering, is only one of the
prizes of Le Mans. Victory in each class carries great prestige,
leading (the makers hope) to increased sales, even more so
twenty years ago perhaps than now.

So unperturbed, imminent lapping or not, Lance Macklin
pressed on towards White House corner and the pits on that
sunny evening of Saturday, June 11, 1955. He was a matter of
seconds – less than a minute – from the greatest disaster in the
history of motor racing. When those seconds had ticked away,
a train of events would start that would mean the death of
eighty-two people, events in which Macklin himself would be

11

one of the principal actors; in which death would at once reach out for and relinquish him. . . .

*　　　　*　　　　*

The 24-hour race is still one of the most glamourous events in motor sport, although its lustre has faded a little outside France. This is because the original conception has been submerged in the engulfing tide of commercial competitiveness. The chief inspiration for its inception more than fifty years ago in 1923 came from Charles Faroux, a tall and impressive patriarchal figure, a man not merely of distinguished presence, but of an influence that for many years until his death dominated French motor racing. The idea was that the race would provide a yardstick of the reliability and quality of motor cars that were being regularly produced – sports and touring cars certainly, but still cars for everyday driving. Nothing lasts for ever (as car buyers know full well). Its very success meant that over the years Le Mans became a very different sort of event. Successful cars meant increased sales – a boost in which everything that went with them shared. Tyres, brakes, oils, batteries, lights, even the barley water or whatever was said to have slaked the thirst of the drivers got the full advertising treatment. And this, by the way, is explanation, not criticism. Nothing lasts for ever! Everything evolves for good or ill.

For good or ill, Le Mans became a race largely for very special cars indeed. Some were really Grand Prix machines with cobbled up 'sports' bodies. 'Prototypes' were permitted. The makers had merely to say that they proposed to produce a given number of them in the future. Alongside these formidable entries were little cars, such as the Panhards with 745 cc engines. This meant that even in 1955 cars capable of nearly 200 mph were hurtling round the circuit together with those barely capable of half that speed. These differences constitute one of the main dangers of Le Mans. But then, motor racing, *all* motor racing, is dangerous.

Now the circuit. If the cars in the race, or many of them, can't be used by the ordinary driver, the eight miles or so on which it is run most certainly can and are. They are public roads, closed for practice and the event, in the Department of

12

Sarthe. Let us drive the circuit (as it was in 1955). We zoom down the Mulsanne straight, the famous stretch (along the four miles of which the aces reach more than 200 mph nowadays) but beware; you come to a hill which conceals an almost immediate right-hand hairpin bend. Round this and up you go towards Indianapolis, so called because a short length of its surface was once cobbled, thus inviting comparison with the famous American track, known as the brickyard. Through the corner here, and then comes the sharp right-hander at Arnage. Now a fast, gently curving couple of miles to the White House, but with one dangerous point, a corner again hidden until you have crested a hill. White House corner won't bother you unless you are foolhardy enough to imagine that you are racing – in which case it is deceptive and tricky. Past White House, then. Ahead is a fast stretch leading to the grandstands on the left and the pits on the right. And since you are driving on one of the most famous circuits in the world, how can you fail to imagine the stands and the enclosures packed with eager, intense crowds yelling as you swoop past, while from one of the pits, your pit, comes a ghostly signal that the Ferraris are hot on your tail. Under the Dunlop Bridge into a long right-hand bend you go, and then a stretch of rather more than half a mile is followed by a sharp left-hander, then a right, and almost at once, another right at Tertre Rouge, and you are back on the Mulsanne straight . . . which is also the road to Tours.

There is one thing to remember as you drive away. Gentle curves and easy corners taken, say, at 60 mph, become tight and difficult at 150.

Le Mans is a somnolent provincial market town that bursts into life in the week of the 24-hours. The townspeople move into caravans, sheds and garages, and let every possible room in their homes to the polyglot invading hordes of racegoers. They pour in, more than 300,000 of them, not merely from all over France, but from all over the world. If you had not made provision the year before, you would be hard put to it find a bed for miles around. Special trains with sleeping coaches pull in and stay until it is all over so that passengers use them as hotels.

Around the circuit itself an army of tents springs up. Behind

13

the pits is a miniature town called the Village. Here there are kiosks and marquees by the hundred. You can buy a car there or get yourself shaved. You can get a meal. You can get drunk. Great canvas booths are set up inside which bands on platforms blare away while the patrons sit on benches at long rough wooden tables drinking steins of beer, mainly, singing lustily in a euphoric outpouring of raucous bonhomie. Through the tobacco haze and the fug of herded humans, take a look at the band. Like as not they'll be wearing leather jerkins and *lederhosen*. So will the sweating, scurrying waiters. Or if girls are doing the job they'll be in square and low-cut – but highly interesting – bodices and full sweeping skirts that are called (to the best of my information) dirndls. I have gone into this detail because I have never understood the Bavarian influence in the matter of the Le Mans beer tents. At any rate, it is a manifestation of Franco-German accord. When you have drunk enough, you can wander into the fairground. At night the Big Wheel is a brilliantly lit landmark. On the other side of the track, behind the grandstands, are full-scale restaurants, and dotted about the area are almost as many enterprises for parting the customers from their cash as in the Village. Circus shows, strip booths, shooting galleries, *crêpes* stalls lit at night by gaudy naphthalene flares. Whole families come for what is really a festivity. Behind earthen embankments concealing the circuit, they picnic and their children romp. Lovers stroll or lie together with eyes and ears only for each other as the unseen, irrelevant cars roar by. At night the headlights penetrate the dark in sudden, almost shocking, stabs of light. And on Sunday morning Mass is said in the open. A good many of the 300,000 leave their cars (there are 373 acres of car parks) on Saturday morning and drive them out again on Sunday evening without ever having seen any of the racing.

*   *   *

Pat Mennem, in 1955, as now, motoring reporter of the *Daily Mirror*, did not find it all that easy to get to Le Mans. The News Desk weren't too keen for him to go. 'In those days,' he recalls, 'we weren't frightfully interested in motor racing.' But at the last minute it was decided that he should cover the race after all. 'In those days, of course, it was one of the big motoring events of the year, and capable of leading the paper as it did in 1953 when the British team of Tony Rolt and Duncan Hamilton won in a C-type Jaguar. I flew to Normandy and got a train to Le Mans. I didn't have anywhere to stay, it was impossible to get into a hotel, it was almost impossible to get into a private house, but in the end I found a room. This was my third Le Mans. I'd been there a couple of times before for the *Coventry Evening Telegraph,* but the whole atmosphere of Le Mans never loses its impact. They talked of half a million being there. Well, there were certainly three hundred thousand. It was a weekend *en fête*, a great occasion to the French. And for the British a great occasion too, because we used to do quite well there in those days.'

Erik Johnson a cub reporter on the *Oxford Mail* by profession, and a motor racing *aficionado* by inclination, was hoping to combine business with pleasure. He hadn't been married all that long, but the pull of motor racing was strong. He and his father and a couple of friends were spending a holiday driving to races on the continent. It was the year that the MGs came back to racing. They were built in Oxfordshire. And they had a team entered for Le Mans. 'I kidded the chief reporter,' says Johnson, 'into letting me apply for Press facilities – on the basis that I would be there on holiday anyway – so that if anything interesting happened to the MGs, if they did well, I could write about it for the paper. But really I was there mainly for my own enjoyment.

'It was very hot that Saturday afternoon when we got to the circuit. I remember it was a long, hot summer, '55. We arrived after a lot of queueing to get into the car park. Then we walked to an area near the bend not far from the grandstand. It was six or eight deep in people up against a chestnut fence. We could see nothing over the heads of the crowd there, so we moved on. . . .'

To that patch of ground (if they were not already there) came two other young Englishmen. One was Jack Diamond, from Edgware, London, who ran a garage. Neighbours often saw fast cars outside his house. He went to as many of the big races as he could. The other was Robert Loxley of Worcester. They did not move on. A couple of doctors, Geoffrey Dickson

15

and Duncan McDermott, from the Western Hospital in London's Hammersmith, were in the stands. They were there as racing enthusiasts, not medical men.

Jacques Ickx, the distinguished Belgian motoring writer (father of Jacky, the brilliant present-day Grand Prix driver who won Le Mans in 1969, in 1975 and in 1976) was there as a reporter. Tommy Wisdom; veteran motoring journalist and driver, was there to report the race for the *Daily Herald* – in between spells of driving, at the age of 48, a Bristol in the event. François Jardell, a young Frenchman with driving ambitions, had brought a girl friend from Paris. He stood near the pits, watching the activity and wishing that he himself was getting ready to drive. One day, perhaps . . .

In and around the pits the tension mounts. It is time to look at some of the men who will soon be racing, and at some of those who run the teams.

The Mercedes-Benz entry of three silver 300 SLRs is remarkable. They are the first cars to race at Le Mans with fuel injection. In one respect they are not so advanced as their main rivals. They have brake drums instead of discs. But they have a strange device to counter this. A lever touched by the driver raises or lowers a metal flap behind him. It is designed to act as an air brake. During practice other drivers objected that these obscured their vision in the corners, so Mercedes have cut windows in them with transparent plastic screens. And in the cockpit are four plungers which the driver can press to lubricate any brake drum which may be binding.

The Mercedes are formidable not only because of their splendid design and their superb 2975 cc engines, but also because of the calibre of their No. 1 crew. In the history of motor racing three drivers are generally regarded as having been the greatest ever. The Italian Tazio Nuvolari; Juan Manuel Fangio of the Argentine; and Britain's Stirling Moss. The legendary world champion Fangio and Stirling Moss are sharing the driving of a Mercedes. The other two are driven by the German Karl Kling and André Simon of France, and the veteran Frenchman Pierre Levegh with John Fitch, an American.

Moss, the brilliant, mercurial and sometimes choleric Moss, with an incredible string of victories in all kinds of racing to

16

his name, does not care much for the 24-Hour Endurance Race of Le Mans.

He told me with all the Moss bluntness: 'I think there is more bullshit spoken about Le Mans than any other race. And if you look at the history of Le Mans, the interesting thing is that it has never been won by a great driver. Ever. The best driver who has won Le Mans was Mike Hawthorn. He was good. But there has never been a great winner, a Nuvolari or a Fangio, or even a Jackie Stewart or a Jimmy Clark. I don't think Le Mans requires great driving ability. It requires great stamina. It requires great discipline. Those who have won it, like Olivier Gendebien and Maurice Trintignant and Phil Hill, were terrific drivers and particularly suited mentally and physically for that event. They could pace themselves and control themselves. They were not men given particularly to fiery performance, because fire and Le Mans don't mix. It is not a passionate race. You see, you cannot *race* . . . There's no man alive who can sprint 100 yards – and keep it up for a mile. There's no man alive who can race a Grand Prix for three hours and keep it up for twenty-four. No. There's no passion in it. It's a heartless race. When I signed my contract with Maserati, later than '55 it is true, I had Le Mans left out. Yes, I *would* drive there, but only because driving was my business. But I would make sure that I was well paid for it. I would drive in a Grand Prix virtually for nothing if I had to, but I wanted a lot to go to Le Mans because I didn't enjoy it and I didn't think that it was a test of my skill.'

In the Mercedes pit are the racing manager Alfred Neubauer, an elderly, portly figure with a famous outsize homburg from which he seemed inseparable, Rudolph Uhlenhaut, a first-rate driver, who had done much of the development and design work on the cars, and Artur Keser, public-relations chief. This is a key job. For Mercedes set the greatest possible store by their public image and this is destined to become a matter of high drama before the end of this Le Mans.

Over to the Jaguar pit. Already there is the shadow of tragedy here. The son of company chief William Lyons has been killed driving to Le Mans.

Jaguars are entering three D-types. The No. 1 driver is Mike Hawthorn, a tall, blond, dashing hell-of-a-fellow. We find him wearing the inevitable dotted bow tie for which the French call him The Butterfly. On his day he is a match and more for the best in the world. Sharing his car is the burly, moustached Ivor Bueb. Then there are the old faithfuls, Rolt and Hamilton, winners two years previously. The third car is in the hands of Don Beauman, whom Hawthorn would have preferred to Bueb as his co-driver, and Jaguar's chief tester Norman Dewis, now being given a chance to show what he can do in a big race. There are also two privately entered cars. One crew are the Americans, Walters and Spear; the other are the Belgians, Swaters and Johnny Claes. As well as being a fine driver, Claes is well known as a jazz musician. He runs a band, Johnny Claes and his Clay Pigeons. Both these cars have works support.

Running things in the pit is one Frank Raymond Wilton England, all of 6 ft 5 in., and known therefore as Lofty. At this time Lofty England is 44, and there isn't much about racing and running a racing team that he doesn't know. While still at school he had his first real encounter with the internal combustion engine in the shape of a 1921 Douglas motor cycle which he bought for £10. (A well-heeled schoolboy, evidently; £10 was a lot of money in the twenties.) After school came a five-year apprenticeship with Daimler's London service department. Then he moved on to a job where, among other things, he prepared racing cars, including Sir Henry Birkin's $4\frac{1}{2}$-litre supercharged Bentley for its appearances at Brooklands of nostalgic memory. Then he became racing mechanic to the millionaire Whitney Straight, who was running a team of Maseratis, and from there to the racing-car firm of ERA, and then to work with the famous Bira, the motor-racing Prince Birabongse of Siam. He did some racing himself, mainly motor cycles in the Isle of Man and Brooklands. Lofty was second in the 1936 lightweight Manx Grand Prix, riding a 250 Rudge-engined Cotton. Between 1932 and 1938 he covered the motor-racing scene all over Europe and in North and South Africa. Came the war, and Lofty volunteered for the RAF. He completed his training in the United States and then was loaned to the Americans as a flight instructor. Back in Britain in 1943, he regularly flew Lancasters on daylight-bombing missions against Germany. The war over, he was back to motor cars and to racing. He led at the start of one of the first post-war

18

Grand Prix races, at Brussels in 1946. Towards the end of the race he was lying third when mechanical trouble pushed his Alvis down to sixth place. At the end of that year he joined Jaguar as service manager. Later he was also given the job of managing the works racing team. It was under his direction that some of Britain's greatest victories on the circuits were achieved. A formidable character, then. Dedicated and efficient, prickly and forceful. His aim now as he directs preparations: to win Le Mans.

Let us move on. Here at the Ferrari pit is Eugenio Castellotti watching the final touches being put to his 4½-litre Ferrari. Le Mans always inspires the Italian team to supreme effort. And here is the 1,100 cc Coventry-Climax-engined Lotus and its drivers, Ron Flockhart and Colin Chapman. With them is a young man named Peter Jopp who is here as reserve. It is their first Le Mans for all three. Move on to the 3-litre Aston Martin to be driven by Peter Collins and Paul Frere. Keeping going among the great cars and the great names. What's this? It's the smallest car in the race and the most bizarre. The 735 cc Nardi. It is in the shape of a couple of torpedos. In one of these tubes sits the driver. In the other sits the engine.

Now we look in at the Austin-Healey 100S. It is a works car, owned by its designer, Donald Healey, but it is down as a private entry in the name of its No. 1 driver, Lance Macklin. The reason, explains Macklin (twenty years later) was that in the previous Le Mans 'Healey had withdrawn his cars at the last minute as a protest against all the prototype cars in the race. He said that Le Mans had deteriorated into a Grand Prix for cars with special bodies. Makers were building special cars for the race, while those Donald was racing were more or less production cars. I was supposed to be driving for him when he withdrew the car. In 1955 he wanted the car to race at Le Mans but he thought that the organisers might not accept his entry, and he wasn't going to ask them, anyway. So he asked me, "as you are fairly well known to the organisers, could you get an entry as a private individual?" I had no trouble at all. I asked Les Leston to drive with me.'

It was Leston's first Le Mans. He might have been driving with Hawthorn instead of Bueb. 'Ivor and I were great mates,' he told me. 'We both did a test for Jaguar. We went to Silver-

19

stone and Lofty England tried us both out. Ivor was faster than me, so he got the drive in the Jaguar team.'

Les Leston came out of the RAF in 1945 and a year later hadn't made up his mind what he was going to do with his life. 'I was trying to decide whether to go into the family business which was involved in aircraft instruments or go back to being a professional musician. I was a drummer with the famous Ambrose – Ambrose's Octet, playing with George Shearing, the great jazz pianist, and Teddy Foster, the trumpeter, and people like that, before joining up.

'I was having a weekend at Brighton, and I saw an advertisement for a hill climb at a place called, I think, Stanmer Lodge. I'd never been to one. Somebody talked me into going. I remember one of the cars competing was a thing called a Fuzzi, driven by a character named Lance Macklin. Another car there was a Cooper, which was two Fiat 500s stuck together. The fellow driving that was S. Moss. There were other names, like Reg Parnell and Bob Gerrard. They didn't mean much to me at the time. But I remember that the guy on the microphone said that the previous week this fellow Stirling Moss had been at a hill climb, the first one after the war, at Luton Hoo, and – it was during the days of petrol rationing – the police tried to arrest everyone for misusing petrol. Anyway, Moss had gone out and got fastest time of the day in his Cooper.

'So I got interested in racing cars, and within a couple of years I acquired an SS100 which I drove in a couple of events. Then I met a fellow called Ken Gregory (later famous as Stirling Moss's manager). This was about 1950. He talked me into buying a motor car called a Kieft. It was a sports car that you could buy and race straightaway without needing too much doing to it. It was the first one ever made that I bought, a 500. I entered a race at Blandford Camp in Dorset. I don't think I finished. Then I did a race at Brands Hatch, and one or two more around the place, and realised that the car was no good. It would never go in a straight line, even if I could, and I wasn't too good at that at the time. So then I met a chap called Alf Bottoms, a speedway rider, who had designed and built some cars. I decided to buy one. Peter Collins bought one, too, and we became a sort of team. And in my next year of racing I started winning a few.'

20

Leston didn't stay in the family business. Nor did he ever beat a drum in anger after the war. He decided that what he wanted to do was race.

And now he stands in the Healey pit with Macklin – who, as No. 1 driver, will take the first spell at the wheel, waiting as the time drags by, for the start of the 1955 Le Mans.

There is still a good deal to be done. Tools and spares are stowed in the cars. Only these are allowed to be used if the cars should be in trouble on the circuit. The petrol tanks have to be emptied. An hour and a half to go. It is time for the cars to be fuelled. The petrol – and no other is allowed – comes from an overhead tank at the back of the pits through pipes and then to hoses attached to high, swivelling arms jutting over the pits. Marshals watch closely to see that nothing is added to the fuel. The petrol supplied and no additives – that is the rule. And when the tanks are full, officials called plombeurs wire up the filler caps and fix in place a seal of lead. The plombeurs alone are allowed to break the seals when cars come in to refuel. If a plombeur finds a seal already broken, however accidentally, the race is over for that car. The seals are renewed, of course, after each official refuelling. Engines are warmed up. The tension rises. Half an hour to go. The cars are brought to their starting positions. Two Morettis on which much preparation has been lavished will not even start. They arrived a minute or two after the proper time and have been disqualified. Two reserve entries take their place. Sixty cars are lined up at an angle opposite the pits. Ten minutes to go. The revving engines have to be switched off. A numbered circle is on the road opposite each car. The drivers have to stand on those circles when the race is started. The Nardi's engine is still being worked on. But it is ready as Count Aymo Maggi, the Italian founder of the Mille Miglia race, who has the honour of starting this Le Mans, takes up his position. Still the crowds pour in. All day the narrow roads leading to the circuit have been jammed. Three hundred thousand. Four hundred thousand. Who knows? At any rate it is certain that there are record numbers here. Count Maggi drops the Tricolour. The drivers sprint across the road, dive into their cars, the engines burst into life, and the cars stream away towards the long right hand bend in an inchoate, jockeying stream.

21

From the packed crowds within visual range comes a giant gasp of released tension that swells into a roar. Everyone who has paid to get in has a ticket on which is a warning about the possible danger inherent in watching the race. But who at this moment thinks of that?

It was Castellotti in the scarlet 4.4-litre Ferrari who got to the Dunlop Bridge first. He was in front at Tertre Rouge, followed by Maglioli in another 4.4 Ferrari. Then came the Jaguars of Hawthorn and Beauman in that order. Fangio had made a start that was pure slapstick comedy. He had leaped into his car – and the gear lever had become trapped in his trouser leg! That wouldn't happen with the tight-fitting overalls worn today. Castellotti came into sight of the start-finish line, then was gone, 200 yards ahead of the pack – in which Hawthorn had got past Maglioli into second place. A gap. Then came Walters, followed by Beauman and Jacques Swaters. After those three Jaguars came Pierre Levegh's Mercedes, Roy Salvadori's Aston, Reg Parnell in the big Lagonda, Collins (Aston), Musso (Maserati), Kling (Mercedes), Trintignant (Ferrari), and then the Mercedes of Juan Manuel Fangio. The leaders had completed the first lap. Castellotti's standing start lap had taken only 4 min. 31 sec. It was clear that the early pace, at any rate, was going to be scorching.

Beyond the immediate surrounds of the circuit, families sat on the grass, drowsing in the hot sun, watching the children play, balding fathers surreptitiously eyeing the chic young girls on the arms of boy friends, all only half-aware, through the roaring of the engines, that the great race had started.

The end of the second lap saw Castellotti breaking the record in a time of 4 min. 16 sec. This meant a speed of 117.9 mph. (We are writing of 1955, remember.) Next came Hawthorn, Maglioli and Walters who was right on Maglioli's tail. Fangio, the World Champion, had incredibly moved up from fourteenth to sixth place. Three laps. Fangio was now fourth. The pace was growing hotter. The fourth lap ended with Hawthorn close behind Castellotti. A thirty-second gap, then came Fangio, third. On the tenth lap Fangio shattered the so-recently set up record with 4 min. 10.8 sec. The crowd were enthralled as the three leaders drew ahead of the rest. Fangio passed Hawthorn in front of the stand on the twelfth lap. At the end of an hour's racing the leading cars had covered – for the first time at Le Mans – almost fourteen laps. And Hawthorn was ahead of Fangio again. The leaders were: Castellotti, Hawthorn, Fangio, Maglioli, Walters, Kling, Levegh, Beauman, Rolt and Mieres (Maserati).

Ten minutes later first Hawthorn and then Fangio passed Castellotti. Only a second separated them. At the minnow end of the race the strange twin-boomed Nardi spun at Mulsanne corner and again at Arnage where it went off the road. There it stayed, the driver walking unhurriedly in the direction of his pit, his race run. It is doubtful if many of the spectators remarked its absence or cared if they did. All attention was on the battle for the lead. It seemed clear that the leaders were trying to break each other up, perhaps, almost certainly on instructions. If you overtaxed your most dangerous rival's car, and your own in doing so, then that left the other cars in your team to clean up. After all, it *was* a 24-hour endurance race. Hawthorn and Fangio succeeded with Castellotti's Ferrari. It began to fall back. The lap record went again and again. Those at the back of the crowds strained on tiptoe. The pit counters were packed. Inside the pits were crowded men and women guests of the car makers with the champagne flowing. Too many gatecrashers attempted to share this bountiful hospitality, so the rear entrances of some of the pits were bolted. If the champagne was good, the racing was better. On the eighteenth lap there was a tremendous moment. Fangio got past Hawthorn under the Dunlop Bridge, the Jaguar going into a slide. But Hawthorn passed him on the Mulsanne straight.

Writing of the race* when Fangio was 100 yards ahead, Hawthorn said: 'I suppose I was momentarily mesmerised by the legend of Mercedes superiority. Here was this squat silver projectile, handled by the world's best driver, with its fuel injection and desmodromic valve gear, its complicated suspension and its out-of-this-world air brake. It seemed natural that it should eventually take the lead. Then I came to my senses and thought: Damn it, why should a German car beat a British car? As there was no one in sight but me to stop it, I got down to it and caught up with him again.'

* *Challenge Me The Race* by Mike Hawthorn (Kimber) 1958 and 1975.

23

Hawthorn and Fangio were each lapping at over 120 mph. On the twentieth lap Fangio turned in a time of 4 min. 8 sec. to re-pass the Jaguar. But on the next lap Hawthorn was back in front. Fangio's superb driving skill was being stretched to its utmost. He did get past Hawthorn. And he stayed in front for three laps. Then Hawthorn smashed the record yet again on lap 28 with a time of 4 min. 6.6 sec., 122.393 mph, and there he was, leading the race again.

When it had been going on for two hours the leaders were: Hawthorn, Fangio, Castellotti, Maglioli, Kling, Levegh, Walters, Rolt, Beauman and Musso.

Fangio, Hawthorn. Hawthorn, Fangio. The lead kept changing. Sometimes their cars were wheel to wheel as they raced up past the pits, a narrow part of the circuit. Fangio was touching something over 181 mph down the Mulsanne. Hawthorn was quicker through the corners. This was not a 24-hour endurance race. Nothing like it. This was a Grand Prix, a race that's over in three hours, in cut and thrust and urgency and competitiveness, with the adrenalin flowing.

Flowing, too, was the beer in the tents where the serious drinkers were beginning to get down to it. There was no hurry, though. The hours of Le Mans stretched invitingly ahead. The bands struck up their songs. Waiters and the low-bodiced girls scurried to and fro with trays impossibly balanced. No, no hurry at all. The atmosphere was thickening. But outside, the sun shone in a blue June sky. And the committed lovers, and the merely tentative young men looking hopefully at the girls they had persuaded to Le Mans, wandered around, equally oblivious to the drama on the track, merely waiting for the night.

Not long after six o'clock François Jardell left the pits for a spot the other side of the track. He was supposed to meet his girl there and bring her back for a look at the pits. There – he saw her in the crowd. He stopped to chat to a journalist friend, then began making his way towards her. A few minutes earlier Les Leston had left the Austin-Healey pit which was at the far end of the row, towards the Dunlop Bridge, with a restricted view in the direction of the White House because of the bend in the road. He recalls: 'I was due to take over from Lance Macklin, probably in twenty or twenty-five minutes. I was all dressed up ready. I wanted to see what was going on, and I went down to pit number three – I think it was – and I stood on top of the pits, because from there in those days you could see right the way down the road. You could see White House, anyway, with a little bit of a kink there.' So he stood, looking down towards the White House.

At this point it was the intoxicating battle of Mercedes against Jaguar that was the focus of all eyes. Castellotti was more than a minute behind Hawthorn and Fangio. The Mercedes cars of Kling and Levegh, in that order, were nearly four minutes behind. It could not be long before they would be lapped. Soon, too, the cars would have to be refuelled. Signals to that effect were out in the pits of the three leaders. On the thirty-fourth lap Castellotti came in. The pit erupted into a burst of swift, disciplined action. A minute and a half was all it took before the Ferrari roared back into the race with Marzotto at the wheel. Hawthorn was a fraction over seven seconds ahead of Fangio on their thirty-fifth lap. He passed Levegh, to lap him, just after the White House. Ahead of him, on the straight to the pits, was Macklin. The race had been going on for just over two hours, twenty-five minutes.

Mike Hawthorn, Lance Macklin, Pierre Levegh. They were the three principal actors in a supreme tragedy. In themselves they epitomise a whole vanished era. It is time to look closely at these men.

Macklin

There were, after the end of World War One, a number of institutions that, flourishing still in a threatened social order, reassured traditionalists that come war, come peace, come what may elsewhere, all was well in dear old solid and unchanging England. One such, in a minor way, was the morning parade (if the sun were benign and the winds not too strong) of the off-spring of the well-to-do in perambulators pushed by their female attendants, known as Nannies, in London's fashionable Kensington Gardens. The more gleaming and resplendent the equipage, the more starched the Nanny, the greater were supposed to be the affluence and social standing of their families. And if you chanced to stroll in the Gardens one fine day in, say, 1920, the odds were that the occupant of one pram would have been Lance Macklin, 2 years old, from nearby Gloucester Road.

He was the middle of three children. The others were girls, eighteen months older, and a year younger. His mother was a remote figure. His father was a remarkable man. Noel Campbell Macklin was invalided out of the Army after what his son calls 'a very unpleasant experience which he only just survived'. He was not an engineer in the formal sense, but he had been driving cars since around 1910, and knew as much about them as anybody. Casting around to see what he should do with his life, what more natural than that he should decide to build motor cars? First he launched a machine called the Eric-Campbell, intended for the sporting driver and capable of all of 65 mph. Then he quit his firm, and in 1920 produced a new car, the Silver Hawk. This was an out-and-out sports car with a snappy two-seater aluminium body, outside exhaust pipe and all. It lasted about a year. And then came an extraordinary interlude that gives some idea of the flavour of the man.

Noel Macklin took his family off to Monte Carlo. 'We went there,' says Lance, 'because my father had an idea for a gambling system. Nowadays people using computers have done or attempted similar things, but then it was revolutionary. It was a purely mathematical exercise for him. There is to this day a record printed in Monte Carlo showing every number that comes up on one roulette table in the Casino from the time they open at ten o'clock in the morning until they close at night. He believed that roulette was purely a matter of the laws of probability and chance, and if you knew what had come up for several years, you could plot a chart showing the rise and fall of various combinations.

'He rented a villa for about a dozen people, bought the records for some years back, and worked out his system. He set up an operations room. The walls were covered with graphs, and he could predict virtually exactly what was going to happen in the way of sequences, runs of colours, evens and odds. He employed people to gamble for him at the Casino. They had lists of what to back each day.'

The Monte Carlo episode lasted about a year and a half. Noel Macklin made no great fortune, but that had not been his intention, although he had been able to keep his family and the villa establishment going on the proceeds of his system. He decided that he had done what he had set out to do, which was to prove his point to himself. Then he packed up and returned to England to produce another new car.

The family moved to a new home in Cobham, Surrey, not far from Brooklands, and the car that Macklin built – in workshops at the back of the house, like the great Ettore Bugatti – was the Invicta, of cherished memory among the elder *cognoscenti*. Its sustained capacity for high-speed cruising made the early Invicta a legend. In 1933 the equally legendary Donald Healey won the Monte Carlo Rally in one.

It was no wonder that Lance became interested in cars at a very early age. He spent much time wandering around the workshops. 'My father was a charming, though self-centred man. With my mother things were not quite so easy. She was

27

terribly tied up with my father. Madly in love with him. She fell in love with him when they first met, and she still is to this day, although he has been dead nearly thirty years. She had very little to do with her children. We were brought up almost entirely by governesses and Nannies, and we hardly ever saw our parents. We would be brought down on a Sunday, be presented to the family, if you can imagine it, sing a little song, recite a little piece of verse, and then be whisked back to the nursery. A curiously Victorian atmosphere lingered into the twenties in our home.

'And then, having been brought up in this way with two sisters, governesses and Nannies, I was suddenly shipped off to prep school at Camberley. It was the most horrific day of my life when I found myself abandoned like that. I was 8 years old. I had been snatched from a pleasant country house into a world of horrible, screaming, nasty little boys of around my own age. Most of them knew each other. I was one of the few new boys that term. I remember vividly my first night in the dormitory, one of fifteen boys. I was sitting on my bed, longing for the lights to go out so that I could cry and go to sleep, and some nasty little boy suddenly said to me, "What's your name?" I said, "Macklin," and he said, "What's your Christian name?" and I said, "Lance." "What, Lawrence?" "No, Lance." "What's Lance?" "Lance is short for Lancelot." He could hardly believe his ears. "Lancelot! Gosh, we've got a Sir Lancelot here!" I'd never considered my name as particularly funny. Nobody had ever suggested that there was anything odd about it before. And then some other nasty little boy said, "Do you believe in Father Christmas?" and I said, "Yes." And of course there was a scream of laughter. So obviously I had said something wrong. And then, luckily, the lights went out, and I was left to cry quietly on my own. But I acclimatised myself very quickly. Boys are very tough at that age, and in fact I got on very well, and enjoyed prep school. And of course I went home from time to time, and I used to go to Brooklands with my father when he was running Invictas. They competed in a lot of races, and my feeling for motor racing grew.

'My grandfather had been to Eton. My father had been to Eton. So I went to Eton. I wish I hadn't. I wasn't really cut out for Eton. Why not? It's difficult to say. But I think that I have a French side to my character. I had a French grandmother – my mother's mother. I believe the French wouldn't stomach Eton. I can't think of any French person who would. It's a matter of having to subjugate yourself to that sort of discipline, the weight of tradition. I found it very difficult. Armed neutrality? No. Most of the time it was more like a pitched battle with the authorities. I survived it, but only just. My Eton days were some of the most miserable of my life.

'The one good thing for me was that I loved games, and Eton is a wonderful school for that. I wasn't ever brilliant at any particular game, but I was probably slightly above average at a lot of them. I played squash and fives, and I didn't do badly at boxing. I was very light, paperweight or flyweight, luckily, because I could never really get hurt. My reactions were very quick, so I could stay out of trouble, and I could usually give a reasonable account of myself.'

Cambridge would normally have been the next step for a likely lad from Eton, but Macklin senior considered his son's career at Eton, shuddered at the thought of him going on to university, so Lance found himself at a college in Villars in Switzerland, 4,000 feet up in the Alps, to take a business course and learn foreign languages. And then, father hoped fondly, the boy would come home and take his place in the business. Now if you are a bright young man who has just been released from what you regard as an unmerited stretch in prison, there are worse places to find yourself than Villars, 4,000 feet up in the Swiss Alps. All the same, Villars was not without its problems, as Lance Macklin explains:

'It's a winter sports resort, so I had great opportunities for ski-ing. But I got there in October, and like all winter sports resorts in October, it was dead. All the place could boast was a couple of cafés. There was hardly a soul about. I thought, "What the hell am I going to do now?" I had been at the college a fortnight when I found the answer. A road ran past the top of the college grounds, and I was standing there when a couple of very attractive girls walked past. I hadn't seen a girl for months. I was only about seventeen, and I was beginning to take a keen interest in girls. So I said to one of the fellows with me, "Good heavens, where did they come from?" "Oh," he said, "they're from the finishing school." "Tell me more," I urged. "There's a girls' finishing school called Prantanier just down the road." A few seconds later another couple of girls came by, and then two or three more. I said to my friend: "What do we do about this, then? Do we have any sort of relationship with these girls?" "No." It was high time, I thought, that we did. So I asked our Head: "Don't you think it would be a good idea if we got in touch with the girls' school down the road and organised a dance?" The Head, an Englishman named Mr Barnard, was somewhat sceptical. "I don't think it likely that you can arrange it. But if the girls' Headmistress agrees, then it's all right with me." That was enough for me. I went off to the girls' school and plucked nervously at the bell. I spoke fluent French, and taking some slight licence with the truth, told her that the Headmaster of my college had suggested it would be a good idea if we held a dance, and perhaps some of her girls might come along. She thought it was a marvellous idea.

'The dance was highly successful. I chatted up one of the girls and arranged to meet her next day in a back-street café, which was strictly illegal. Girls weren't supposed to meet young men outside the school. But one meeting led to others. One day I asked her: "Whereabouts in the school is your room?" She said: "My bedroom's on the ground floor. Unfortunately it's next to the Headmistress's study." That didn't deter me. I used to sneak out of college after lights out, climb down an apple tree, go through some woods, dart across the lawn of the girls' school, find my friend's window, squeeze in, and spend a cosy hour or so with her. It was all very innocent, not a question of making love or anything like that, just a little cuddle. It went on for quite a while. It got to the stage where I would spend quite a few hours in her room, in her bed, in fact, but even then it was only a question of a little mild fumbling. I was too young to really make love to her. Like most boys of that age, I had a funny sort of inhibition about making love to girls at that time. Anyway, I woke up one night in this girl's bed. It was about 2 am. I dressed hurriedly and went to step out of the window. Here was drama. There were about six inches of snow on the lawn.

'In the morning the Headmistress walked into her study next to the girl's room. From her window she saw my footprints across the lawn and into the woods. So she promptly asked the girl, "How do you explain this?" And she couldn't really explain very clearly. My footprints were traced back until it was pretty obvious that they came from my college. We were threatened that unless the culprit owned up everybody would be punished. The swift upshot was that I was sacked. Mr Barnard told me: "I'll put a call through to your father to tell him of your expulsion, and I'll let you know what he wants you to do." I thought, I'd better circumvent this. So I put a call through to my father from the post office in the village and told him what had happened. He didn't say anything very much. No reproaches. He didn't laugh.

'What he did say was that Nada, my elder sister, had just finished her deb season in London, she had been going out an awful lot, and had developed chest trouble, and the doctors had just advised that she should go to Switzerland. So before I could ask what he wanted me to do, he told me that Nada was coming over, that I was to find a small hotel and act as a chaperon. I found a little hotel and poor Mr Barnard didn't have a chance to tell my father that he was expelling me. My father simply told him, "I have spoken to Lance, and I understand the position, and thank you very much."

'The girl was sacked too. We met again briefly about twenty years later. I was introduced to Mrs somebody or other at a cocktail party in London. "Lance Macklin," she said. And a great grin spread over her face. "Does Villars before the war mean anything to you?" "Yes, of course. I was at college there." And then it dawned on me who she was. I don't think either of us had laughed so much for years.

'Nada came out, and I must confess that I didn't do much in the way of chaperoning. I spent the days ski-ing and the nights going to bars and clubs. I ran through my money very quickly and I composed a desperate plea that I thought might touch my father's heart and wallet. I wired: *No mon. No fun. Your son.* His immediate response was another wire: *Too bad. How sad. Your dad.* And no money. But he did come across with some a little later.

'I was having a great time. I met a little girl, Josette, Swiss-Italian, seventeen years old, and very attractive. Being Italian she knew so much more about sex than I did. I was still very gauche and inexperienced. She was the first girl who taught me that sex could be fun and interesting and exciting. I fell in love with her. The only problem was that her father was madly possessive about her, and wouldn't even concede that she could go out with anybody. She was staying in a flat with her mother. At weekends when her father was around I had to keep out of the way in case he saw us together.

'Nada met the Comte Jean de Caraman at Villars and fell madly in love with him. When she went home and told my father that she wanted to marry a French Count, he was horrified. Like many Englishmen of his time, he had a vague belief that Frenchmen generally were philandering scoundrels, and the French aristocracy even more so. But despite my father's objections she married her Count.

'I continued to meet Josette after we left Villars. We saw each other in the South of France a couple of times, and she came to England and met my family. She started talking about marriage. I didn't want to marry I was beginning to think of other girls. But I found the answer to the problem.

'At that time I was playing a lot of polo. My father was very keen on horses. He had his own racing string at one time. He was eager for me to ride. I used to compete in point to points, and I had six polo ponies. In one match I met three Argentinians. Polo is a great sport in their country. They said that if I went there I could become a real expert. I had a friend who had a ranch out there, and he offered me a job. It seemed a good idea to me since the Argentine was a long way from everything. It was an opportunity to get away from this girl who was set on marriage. My father was very reasonable about it. He thought it would be good for me to get some world-wide experience before settling down to the family business. He said that if I could arrange everything myself, I could go. I told Josette that I was off to play polo. I worked my passage on a cargo boat and took the job on my friend's ranch some 200 miles south of Buenos Aires. I didn't play any polo, but I worked as a gaucho. I was there for nine months and then World War Two broke out. When I got back to England two months later, Josette was in Switzerland. I didn't see her again until after the war.'

*   *   *

32

Lance Macklin, 19 years old, was not due to be called up as a conscript for at least six months. He volunteered for the Navy straight away rather than wait to be 'pushed into the Army', which was where the bulk of conscripts found themselves, and which appealed to him not at all. He found himself, instead, at HMS *Collingwood*, a training establishment at Fareham, Hampshire.

It was, he says, 'quite amusing in a way, because it was my first real experience of the difference between the type of education I'd had and the type of life I'd had, and the ordinary rough and tumble of people in England. Naturally I got my leg pulled a lot because of my lah-de-dah voice. There were times when I was very glad that I knew how to use my fists. Some of the chaps automatically assumed that the way I spoke meant that I was effeminate. They realised their error when it came to punch-ups.

'I spent three months at HMS *Collingwood*, then I was transferred to an ML, a motor launch designed for patrol duty – which was one of the boats built by my father.'

The elder Macklin had been much impressed by an article written in 1937 by a retired admiral whose theme was that in a future war the submarine would be a greater menace to Britain than the bomber plane. We hadn't, said the admiral anything like enough destroyers and suchlike vessels to deal with this danger. Noel Macklin evolved a plan for building anti-submarine boats in large numbers by mass production methods which were then revolutionary for shipping. It involved pre-fabricating parts and assembling them as one assembles model kits nowadays to make planes or battleships. It involved using, of all things, plywood. The Admiralty looked at the idea and turned it down flat.

'Then,' says Lance Macklin, 'the Munich crisis came and things started to look very black. The Admiralty suggested that he should produce an ML with his own money. If it worked, they would buy it. My father didn't hesitate. He built the first one. It cost about £80,000 and he put virtually everything he had into it. It was launched either a fortnight before or a fortnight after we declared war. Virtually the moment it had done its sea trials the Admiralty ordered a further dozen. Before they were completed, the Admiralty ordered a hundred, and before these were ready, they said they wanted all he could produce. They did inshore patrol work and convoy duties, and released destroyers which could go further out to sea and hunt submarines. My father became very friendly with Churchill, who thought the whole scheme was marvellous. He used to ring up and ask him, "How many have you produced today? You know you have top priority, anything you want." They made my father a Director at the Admiralty and gave him a cheque book. He could sign the government cheque for any amount he thought necessary. He once showed me a cheque he had signed for a million pounds for materials. His signature was all that was needed.

'Although I was merely an ordinary seaman, I soon became popular with the base engineers. When one of them had his boat out of action because of engine trouble, he would come to me and ask, "Is there any chance of your having a word with your father to see if he can get us an engine, because we have an important operation tomorow night?" So I'd ring up my father and tell him that we would be one boat short on an operation unless he could get us an engine, and he'd say, "Leave it to me. I'll see what I can do." Sure enough, next day a truck would arrive with an engine.

'For all that his boats were so successful, my father, by his own wish, never made any money out of them. He was knighted, that was all. When he came back from the First World War, very badly wounded, he was upset because so many people who had stayed behind had become millionaires. Some of his friends had been killed in the trenches. He said. "It's quite wrong. Nobody should be allowed to make money out of the war." What he took was £5,000 a year as salary. Not a penny profit.

'The petty officer on my ML for some reason bitterly resented the fact that my father was a VIP. He spent his life trying to catch me out and make things tough. I got into trouble several times. It happened once because a girl friend came down to Portsmouth from London to spend the night with me. The boat was on the River Hamble, so I drove to Portsmouth. We had all-night leave, but we had to be back on board by 7 am. It was eight o'clock at night when I drove into the railway station to pick up my girl friend. At that moment the air-raid sirens began to wail, and as she stepped off the train the bombs started falling. It was clear that we were in for a nasty blitzing as we drove to the Queen's Hotel in Southsea. We were right. It did get very bad. The Luftwaffe dropped something like 1,000 tons of bombs in an hour on Portsmouth.

'I sent her down into the basement that served the hotel as an air-raid shelter of sorts, and I went out to see what I could do. The hotel was on fire. There were fires everywhere around. The hotel had a fire pump and a big tank of water in the garden. They rushed the pump out, shoved the hose in the tank, but the pump wouldn't start. So we formed a chain with buckets. But it was ridiculous – we might as well have squirted soda siphons at the blaze. It was gaining control, and bombs were whistling down. It seemed to me that they hadn't bothered to do much about the fire pump, so I thought I might as well see if I could get it started. I took a couple of the spark plugs out and cleaned them. Then I took the carburettor to pieces and had a look at that. Finally I got it all together again and it started. With the pump in action we got the hotel fire under control.

'Eventually my girl and I got to bed, but we overslept. When I tried to drive out of Portsmouth every road was blocked. You can't believe what it was like. Buildings were down in great heaps across the roads. I reached the boat three-quarters of an hour late. It didn't matter that I had saved the hotel by getting the bloody pump going. That wasn't considered any excuse. I was confined to the boat for a while.

'Not long after that we were mined. At that time we were on convoy duty between Portsmouth and the Thames Estuary. We'd pick up a convoy at base, escort it through the Straits of Dover, and then we'd wait for another convoy going the other way and go back with it. The Straits were very fiercely fought over. The Germans had big gun batteries on the French coast and planes including dive bombers from airfields only a throw away. And they threw everything at each convoy. It was a very tough proposition. But on the night I'm talking about we'd got through the Straits and were breezing along quite nicely believing that we were out of the danger area. I was on the bridge. Suddenly there was the most shattering bang. One moment the top of the funnel had been over my head. The

35

next. I was looking down into it. I had been blown high into the air. The back half of the boat was almost blown off, the engines were torn out of their cradles, and men in the engine room were wounded.

'We managed to get ourselves towed into Sheerness, and the boat was then paid off, and we commissioned another. I don't know whether it was because the authorities thought we'd had a tough enough time on the convoys, but in the new boat we were sent to Fort William in Scotland, where a base was being started up to train future officers. It was nice and quiet there. They had never heard an attacking plane. They had never been shelled. A regular haven.

'While I was there, just about to be charged with some other offence, a signal came through that I was to report to HMS *King Alfred* at Hove, Sussex, to be trained as an officer. The Cox'n – I didn't like him at all, we didn't agree – the Cox'n said to me, "Good luck to you. This is a nice little berth, it will suit me for the rest of the war, and if you want to volunteer for all your bloody stupid things like convoying, that's up to you." A few months later the stoker of the boat I'd left went down into the engine room and started up the generator, and there was an almighty explosion. The stoker was killed. So was the Cox'n.

'I was commissioned as a sub-lieutenant, and then I went into motor gunboats. Again, I volunteered for them. Most of the young men being commissioned seemed to want to go into battleships and cruisers. I found myself in Robert Hichens' flotilla at Felixstowe, the crack motor gunboat flotilla. Robert Hichens – he was killed later – was a fabulous man. He was one of the most decorated people in the Navy. He had the DSO and bar, and the DSC and two bars. Another thing that endeared him to me was that he was keen on motor racing. He had actually driven at Le Mans.

'Although I had been riding in point to points and playing polo before the war, I wanted more than anything to be a racing driver. I remember before I went to the Argentine there was a little garage in Esher not far from my home which had an Austin 750 cc single-seater in its showroom. I'd seen it race at Brooklands once or twice. I used to see it as I drove past in my little Wolsey Hornet. Eventually I stopped at the garage and talked to the man who owned it. The outcome was that he agreed to hire it to me for a race. We fixed the fee at £15 which I could just about rake up. He said I could practice with it at Brooklands, so I entered it for the race. A Competition Licence? You didn't need one then. All I had to do was send for an entry form with £3 fee for the race.

'The next thing was that Percy Bradley, the Clerk of the Course at Brooklands, rang my father: "I see that we have a Lance Macklin entered at the next meeting. Is he by any chance your son?" My father said, "That's interesting. I didn't know anything about it." "Yes," said Bradley, "he's driving an Austin." "Oh, really? We'll see about that."

'Next morning I went to our garage to pick up the Hornet. It wasn't there. We had a phone in the garage that rang through to our chauffeur's quarters. Sometimes he would take the car out to wash it or fuel it, so I rang him. He said: "Your father told me to lock it up. You'd better speak to him about it." So I went round to my father's office and asked, "What's all this about my car?" And *he* asked, "What's all this about you driving a car in a race at Brooklands?" I told him, and he said: "Not with your allowance from me. If you want to go motor racing, fine. But you make your own money and you pay for your own car. I'm not going to support you in motor racing. Either you cancel your entry and you may have your car back, or you go ahead and make your own way." Of course, I didn't have any way of making money, and anyway I was about to go to the Argentine, so I had to cancel my entry. That was my first effort to go into motor racing.

'It was strange. His Invictas went motor racing, and at one time he was involved in the ERA racing project with the famous Raymond Mays. But he hated motor racing. All his life he was against my motor racing. Anything I wanted to do with horse racing, that was fine. His ambition was for me to ride in the Grand National, which I should think was probably more dangerous than motor racing.

'Anyway, all through the war I was resolved to become a racing driver, and that was why I admired Hichens so greatly. After Hichens I joined another gunboat at Yarmouth, and then I had an exciting spell at Dover which was under constant enemy attack. And then came a great day. I got a signal to report to Shoreham in Sussex to commission my own boat.

'There was this new ML with the finishing touches still being put by the yard – my first command. I came aboard. The First Lieutenant arrived. Then the Cox'n. Finally, after a week, a bus-load of ratings turned up, and there was I with my own boat and crew – two officers, the Cox'n who was a petty officer, and twelve men. You can imagine how proud I was. The Cox'n reported that the crew were on board, and I said grandly: "When they've settled in, muster them and bring them down to the wardroom and I'll interview them one by one."

'A motor gunboat is a very small thing. I heard the Cox'n clattering down the steps and lining the men up in the passage-way outside the wardroom, which is itself pretty cramped. The first rating to come in was the most senior, what is known in the Navy as a Three Badge Able Seaman. Such men have been in the Service at least twelve years, and they are the salt of the British Navy. The Cox'n opened the door, gave the name of this chap, and in he came. He was weather-beaten, with a red face, and his formidable bulk seemed to fill the small room. I was 21. I had been a 10-year-old at prep school when he had joined the Navy. It was incongruous. But I didn't realise it at that moment. I was savouring the situation. My first command. I said: "How do you do? Have you been on small boats before?" "No," came the reply, "I've been on big ships all the time." I nodded sagely. "Well, you may find this a bit different." We chatted for a few moments and off he went. Now on a boat of that size the skipper's personality is highly important to the crew. If he is a reasonable sort of fellow you can, even in those cramped conditions, have a reasonable sort of life. If he is a bastard you can have a hell of a life. Well, when my Three Badge Able Seaman left, I sat back smugly, pleased with the way I'd handled that first interview. Then I heard the others out in the corridor. "What's he like? What's he like?" And I heard, too, the reply: *"Fuckin' schoolboy!"* My ego fell to the deck.

'But I got to know them all very well. And in the end being a fuckin' schoolboy didn't matter much. They knew that I came from Cobham. They also thought that I was a bit mad. So before we went into action they would say: "Now listen, skipper. If you want your name on the Cobham War Memorial, that's up to you. But we don't want ours. We don't want any medals. All we want is leave."

'It was a rough war in those motor gunboats. We were no longer escorting our own convoys through the Straits – we were attacking German convoys. The girls when one got back to Dover were some consolation, of course. During the war one had so many girl friends. They never really lasted long. As a young man one seems to get bored rather quickly with the same girl once you have persuaded her to go to bed with you. You sleep with her half a dozen times – and that's it. The next one is something new on the horizon. That's how it was for me in wartime.

'For me the war was a bore. Perhaps that's not quite the right word. But I hated it. It wasn't what I wanted to be doing. It seemed to me a ridiculous waste of time.' But even the insanity of war had to end. And when it did Lance Macklin was at last free to think about what was then the burning passion of his life. Motor racing.

*   *   *

Before the war, Lance Macklin had heard of a strange character who had built an even stranger motor car. The man's name was Waddei, Robert Waddei. Around 1937 he had taken an idea from Vickers who were the first to use space frames for building planes. The fuselage was in the form of a triangulated space frame. Waddei copied this idea for his design – the first space frame car. It was virtually a fuselage, so he called it the Fuzzi, giving it an extra z. It had four-wheel drive. There were two JAP engines. One drove the front wheels, the other, the rear. The Fuzzi was designed for sprints and a very advanced machine it was. It had independent suspension all round. It had an odd, rocking accelerator pedal. When you pressed the top of the pedal you gave the front engine more power. When you pressed the bottom it boosted the rear engine. If you pressed the whole pedal you gave maximum power to both engines at once. 'It took,' says Macklin reflectively, 'a lot of driving.' Waddei did very well with his Fuzzi, breaking records in hill climbs and sprints and like

39

events. Macklin had never met him until one day during the war.

'He suddenly arrived on my boat in Dover,' says Macklin. 'He said he had come to check the hydraulic steering. At that time the hydraulic steering on MTBs and MGBs was all Lockheed. Waddei was the Lockheed representative. He checked the boat, and then we started chatting. And then I found that he was keen on motor racing and that he was the man who had designed and built this astonishing little Fuzzi. By the time the war ended he had decided not to go sprinting or hill climbing any more, so he agreed to sell me the Fuzzi. I was terribly elated, even though it was just the chassis and body I'd bought. Waddei was always hard up, and he had sold the engines during the war. I got a big Mercury V8 engine, put that in, and drove the four wheels off it. And that was how I first went into motor sport. It was sprinting and climbing. There was no racing immediately after the war.'

Noel Macklin had told his son that if he wanted to be a racing driver, he would have to do it himself, with his own money. Lance didn't go home, didn't go into the family business, didn't take money from father when he left the Navy. With his wartime gratuity, and together with a friend, he started a business called Chipstead Motors in London. He looks back on that time somewhat wistfully. It is a long while since he had any connection with it. And Chipstead Motors which became a very well-known and prosperous firm. It happened this way:

Miraculously, because it was hard to find somewhere to live at all after the war, he found a flat at an absurd rent of £2 a week. 'It was in a mews just off the Gloucester Road where I'd started life. My friend Peter Hodge wanted to start a motor business. He had some £5,000. It wasn't all that much. So I said, "Why don't we use my flat? I've got a living room and a bedroom, a kitchen and a bathroom. We could use the bedroom as an office. And there's a huge garage." And that's how we started Chipstead Motors.

'We had great fun because we decided to buy and sell only sports cars. Nobody drove around in sports cars during the war. They had virtually disappeared. But there were many hidden away in garages and barns in out of the way places. We

40

took out subscriptions for just about every local newspaper we could find. Every day some of these would arrive, and the moment we got them we'd go through them, and every now and again we'd see a sports car advertised in some God-forsaken place. We'd bought an ex-Army Jeep and off we'd dash.'

The ancient Romans had a saying: *Let the buyer beware.* When Macklin and his partner went on their acquisitive raids, *let the seller beware* would have been more appropriate. Nobody who has ever bought a car from, or sold one to, a second-hand dealer will be surprised at the cheerful chicanery that Macklin recalls with a nostalgic twinkle.

'We'd find the car we were after. Sometimes it wouldn't have been started for three or four years. Sometimes it would be standing on blocks, and we'd have to pump the tyres up. We would say to the owner: "Obviously it isn't going to start, so we'll have to tow it away. How much will you accept for it?" We never said that we'd try to start the thing. The owner would reply that he was hoping to get, say, £300. We would assure him that it might cost that much to get someone to try to get it started. In the end we'd settle for, say, £200. We'd make a great thing out of hooking up a tow-rope from the Jeep to our new car, and away we'd go. But only for about half a mile down the road. Out of the seller's sight, we'd stop, put a drop of petrol in the car and try to start it on the button. Nine times out of ten it would start right away. Back in London we'd advertise it for, say, £600.'

Let the buyer beware. Let the seller beware. That was the used-car business. It still is. Even so, you can scarcely call it the unacceptable face of capitalism.

'All the while,' says Macklin. 'I was mad to start motor racing. Couldn't wait. But I hadn't got a racing car, although I was re-building the Fuzzi. All I could do was watch as much motor sport as possible. I used to go with Jon Pertwee, the actor who many years later was to become known to millions as Dr Who on television. I'd met Jon during the war when he was in the Navy. He was keen on motor racing, too. He had a little Frazer Nash in which we went to the sprint events like Shelsley Walsh and Prescott. We devised a very good scheme for watching them. We bought a couple of brooms, and we'd put on work-men's overalls. We would walk quite brazenly through the

41

gates carrying the brooms. Nobody ever questioned us, and we never paid anything. We would walk up to a corner and pretend to sweep gravel away. And when a race started we'd just stand there, leaning on the brooms, watching. Usually we had a marvellous view.

'I remember that we went to France to watch the Grand Prix at Rheims. I'd bought a caravan to take to race meetings and so save on hotel expenses. Jon and I took the caravan to Rheims four or five days before the race, so that there were no officials around, and parked it in a field right next to the circuit, so that we would have a good view.

'We were at a loose end until the race started, so we locked the caravan and decided to head for Paris. We didn't have much money, but a friend had told us: "Go and find a boat on the Seine that belongs to a man called Whizzo Davies. It's a big yacht, and it's being seized by the Customs, but Whizzo is living on board. He has plenty of spare cabins and I'm sure he'll put you up."

'That sounded useful, saving the price of a hotel, so we drove into Paris and along the Seine, and eventually found the yacht and Whizzo. He was very hospitable. "Any friend of Charlie's (or whoever it was that had given us his name) is a friend of mine. Only too pleased." And so saying he led us to a great stateroom, complete with its own bathroom, all very luxurious. "Make yourselves at home," he said pleasantly, and left.

'We went out that night, had a fine, brisk time, returned early next morning and went to sleep ... until we were awakened by a great clattering of feet on the deck above. The feet came rushing down the companion ladder, and the door of our cabin burst open. Three French gendarmes and a couple of men looking like Maigret owned the feet. One of the men looked at me and said, "Monsieur Davies?" I wasn't too clear about anything after our night out and this rude awakening, but I knew that I wasn't Monsieur Davies. So one of the Maigrets turned to Jon. "*Alors* – you are Monsieur Davies?" Jon denied this, but was ready to help. "Down there somewhere," he said. "Down the corridor on the right." The gendarmes and the Maigrets moved out and found Whizzo in his cabin. We heard a lot of excited gabble, and then the whole party moved back up on top and into the wheelhouse and chattered away there.

'We didn't know what it was all about, but felt that it wasn't very healthy. I said, "I think we might as well leave, I'm sure Whizzo will understand." So we packed our little suitcase. Our car was parked on the quay twenty yards from the boat. I said to Jon, "I'll have a look around upstairs, and if there's nobody about, I'll get off, and get into the car. You bring the case up, and if I make a sign that it's all right, come across and we'll drive off."

'I went up, had a look round, and there was one gendarme standing at the other end of the boat. He couldn't see me, so I casually strolled off and got into the car, and started the engine. A few seconds later Jon's head appeared through the hatch. Jon is a natural comedian. He thought the whole situation was terrible funny. He climbed over the guard rail, and then instead of walking across normally, he started to creep around with a sort of ostentatious furtiveness, peering over his shoulder, and so on, and the next thing we knew, there were whistles blowing everywhere and the car was surrounded. We were promptly arrested and marched back to the boat.

'After an hour or so of animated discussion, Whizzo managed to persuade the gendarmes that we had nothing to do with the trouble – which had arisen because he had knocked down part of a bridge on his way up the Seine, and the Customs or water authority were charging an enormous sum for repairs. He didn't have the money, and they had seized the boat and wouldn't let him move it until he paid up. Anyway, one of the Maigrets told us, "Very well, it seems that you are not involved in this regrettable affair. Produce your passports to that man at the door over there, and you may go." I said to Jon, "You have the passports, haven't you?" And he said, "No. You've got them."

'The Maigret-man regarded us without amusement. But the dialogue that ensued was like something out of P. G. Wodehouse.

' "Where are your passports?"
' "In the caravan," I said
' "In the what?"
' "In the caravan." At that time to the French police

43

caravans just meant gipsies. And they didn't care for gipsies or any other sort of nomads.

' "Where is the caravan?"

' "It's in Rheims," Jon said.

' "Where in Rheims?"

' "We're not sure. It's in a field."

'That was the end of that dialogue. We were driven off to the police station and shoved into a room where we sat with a gendarme guarding us. I was pretty worried. I said to Jon, "What are we going to do? You know what they are like in France. They can lock you up for weeks before anything happens." He didn't answer. He was sitting at a desk busily writing postcards which he had bought when we arrived the day before. He thought it would be funny to send them to his friends from a French cell.

'We stayed there quietly until around noon, and we were beginning to feel hungry because we hadn't had any breakfast. So we started to demand our rights. "We want to see the British Consul. We want something to eat." We kept up a clamour until the policeman sitting guard over us said he would see if he could get us some food.

'As soon as the door closed behind the man, Jon said, "Look at this," opened the drawer of the desk and produced a revolver. He said happily, "We can shoot our way out." I said frantically, "For Christ's sake put that bloody thing away. If he comes back and sees you with that, he'll shoot you." Regretfully Jon put the gun back in the drawer. Finally, in the afternoon we were brought before a senior officer who said, "Perhaps this will teach you not to leave your passports behind," and we were released.'

*　　　　*　　　　*

At last Lance Macklin completed his Fuzzi car and got it to the point where he thought it might be competitive. He entered it for several events, but had to cancel each time because the car was not quite ready. Finally, after much frustration, it was. He takes up the story.

'I entered it in a hill climb at a place called Stanmer Lodge, near Brighton. It was my first attempt at competitive motor sport. It was also Stirling Moss's. We both competed for the first time in our careers on the same day, at the same time, at the same event, and I think we both won our class.

'But I was becoming more and more and more frustrated because motor racing, as distinct from hill climbs and sprints, was starting up again after the gap left by the war, and the Fuzzi was not a true racing car.

'A friend of mine, John Gordon, had a Maserati, a 6CL Maserati. I don't know how it had arrived in England. Gordon was looking for someone to put some money up for one or two modifications which were needed on the car, and then race it on a partnership basis. I paid him £800 for a half-share in the Maserati, and we spent some more money on the modifications. And then I entered it for the Isle of Man races which were being organised by the British Racing Drivers' Club. There wasn't such a thing then as a Competition Licence which shows that a driver has had some experience.

'I sent off my entry form with the required £5 fee, and I got a polite, but somewhat curt letter back from Desmond Scannell, then secretary of the BRDC. He asked for details of my experience, because I was proposing to drive a very powerful Formula One car. It was $1\frac{1}{2}$-litres supercharged, which was Formula One at that time. Of course I had to write back that I had virtually no experience. Scannell replied that in that case the Club was very sorry, but my entry could not be accepted.

'You can imagine how I felt. I had spent all the money I had, every penny, on the Maserati, and now I wasn't being allowed to drive it. I was so angry that I rang Scannell and demanded to see him. I stormed into the place, all ready to be rude and aggressive. And there I was, confronted by this charming man who said, "I'm sorry. I really do sympathise with you. But you must see it from our point of view. You are inexperienced. If we authorise you to drive in a race and you cause an accident which kills twenty people, we are going to be blamed for letting you loose."

'It was reasonable, of course. But I was still angry, and I had a point, too. I said, "Well how the hell am I supposed to start racing? The bloody war has been on for the past five or six years. How am I supposed to start? I couldn't race before the war. I've got to start somewhere, sometime!"

'Scannell thought for a moment, then he asked, "Do you have a sports car you can drive? I told him that the only sports car I had was an Invicta, an old car that I had bought through Chipstead Motors. I had got it because of its connection with the past for me, and anyway I thought it would be fun to have an Invicta. Scannell asked, "Does it go all right?" "Yes. Very well." "Would you be willing to race it?" Certainly, I said – if anyone was prepared to accept a 1932 motor car in their event in 1947. It didn't seem that anyone would want to accept me. But Scannell said that he would try to get me entries for the Invicta in one or two places.

'I went away without much hope, depressed and still angry. About a week later Scannell rang and said, "There's a race in Chimay in Belgium in a month's time. If you can get your Invicta over there, I think I can arrange for you to get £50 starting money, which will pay your expenses. They haven't any British entries, and they'd like some. Would you be interested?" Would I be interested, indeed! Of course I would.

'So that was it. I was entered for Chimay. With a friend I set off across the Channel and drove down to the place.

'The sports cars to be reckoned with at that time were the Lago-Talbots, the Delahayes, the Delages, all very modern-looking and streamlined compared to my old Invicta, a 1932 car that had been designed in 1929. It looked ridiculously out of place.

'Chimay was run by a man named, if I remember aright, Buisseret. He ran it independently, in his own way, virtually a law unto himself. It was a very narrow circuit. There wasn't room to have three or four cars side by side on the grid, so they were lined up two and two and two right the way down the road. There was no sophisticated nonsense about practice times determining your starting position. Buisseret, if that indeed was his name, decided which cars were going to be the first pair, and which second and third and so on. I think he did it on the basis of personal distinction. He just said Fangio (or whoever) in front, and Ascari with him, and we'll put Farina and Musso on the second row, and somebody else on the third, until he ran out of people he knew, and then he'd go on how fast the car looked, or some such equally odd criterion.

'All the same, I practised to the fullest extent in my little

Invicta. I knew the car very well; I'd been driving it for a long time. In those days I was so mad keen about motor racing that I used to spend most of my time going round corners sideways, even on the public roads. I'd watched them do it at Brooklands. Not, of course, on the banked track, but on the road circuit they had there. There was also a mountain course. I'd also gone to motor races at Donington and on the Continent before the war, and I saw the top people driving. The big Mercedes and the Auto-Unions used to get themselves drifting through the corners. But one place where I learned more about motor racing than anywhere was Belgrave Square.'

Belgrave Square? Belgrave Square in the heat of London, where the Royal Automobile Club has its motor-sport offices? Yes, indeed!

'In those days it was surfaced with wooden blocks, and the moment it rained, they became so slippery, it wasn't true. And sometimes I'd come out of a night club at around two o'clock in the morning, and it would be pouring. And I'd think "Fabulous!" And I'd leap into the old Invicta and belt round to Belgrave Square. I'd spend ten minutes going round the square in a four-wheel drift all the way. Straight steering and going round on the throttle. You could get up to fifty or sixty miles an hour.

'Anyway, this was Chimay, not Belgrave Square. It was near the French border, and the race was called, grandly, the Grand Prix des Frontières. Not only did M. Buisseret not know me, but my car didn't look very fast, so I was put at the back. I was sitting there at the start of the first race of my life. No crash hat. No racing overalls. Just a short-sleeved shirt, a pair of trousers and a pair of plimsolls. The car in front of me was a Delage. The flag went up. It came down. And the Delage burst into flames. I had been in first gear ready to shoot off. I'd gone forward as the flag dropped. But now I had to stop and go backwards to give myself room to get round the blazing Delage. By this time everybody had streamed on to the narrow track with fire extinguishers. The track was blocked in front of me.

'Eventually I managed to get through. But by then I suppose I had lost half a minute at least on the rest of the field. The whole bunch had gone off in a great screaming roar, and half a minute later round I came in the old Invicta. I could *see* – literally see – the crowd laughing at me. I could see the great grins on the faces as I came into the corners. They didn't know what had happened. They just thought I was half a minute behind already – only halfway round the first lap. I felt so idiotic. I thought, "Oh Christ, I don't want to drive this bloody stupid motor car in this race anyway!" I was furious with Desmond Scannell and the BRDC. I thought, "I'm only doing it because of their bloody ridiculous attitude!" And I went belting on round the corners, and after half or maybe three-quarters of an hour I came into the straight, and suddenly at the end of it I saw a car. I thought, "That's funny. I must be catching somebody up. Well, that's good. At least I must be gaining on someone." Next time round on the straight that car was just a bit nearer. Finally I caught him and overtook him. "Well," I thought, "That's good, I'm not last." And then there was another car not far ahead, so I passed him. And after two or two and a half hours of racing, I climbed into fourth place. This was quite remarkable in the old Invicta. Admittedly one or two people had broken down in front of me, and that helped. Nonetheless, there I was lying fourth and going strong with half an hour to go. Then the battery fell out and that stopped me. It was hung in a cradle under the car. The track was bumpy and the cradle had got rusty, so that the jolting had broken it.

'It wasn't by any stretch of anyone's imagination an important race, but perhaps because there were so few races at this time after the war, there was a journalist from one of the British motoring papers there. He wrote a glowing report about me and my ancient Invicta. He told how I had been baulked at the start for all that time, and despite that, had got to fourth place against some very high-powered opposition. The whole of his report was written about me. It was just what I needed.

'Back in London a couple of weeks later I was in the Steering Wheel Club in Mayfair, and ran into a chap named Ian Metcalfe, whom we called irreverently the Laughing Lavatory Brush. He had a beard, you see. And he laughed a lot. What else could we call him? During the war Metcalfe had bought the Barnato-Hassan 8-litre Bentley which for a short while just before the war had held the lap record at Brooklands –

142 mph or thereabouts. Metcalfe replaced the Bentley's single-seater body with a two-seater body, added four mudguards, a self-starter and headlights, and called it a sports car. Then he entered it for the 24-hour race at Spa, in Belgium. As well as being the entrant, he named himself as No. 1 driver, and put the co-driver down as Mr X. But he couldn't find anyone to drive with him. He approached all the well-known drivers. They said, "You must be mad. A bloody 8-litre track car at Spa, which is the most dangerous circuit in Europe anyway!" That day at the Steering Wheel Club somebody suggested, "Why not ask Lance Macklin? He drove that Invicta at Chimay – didn't you read about it?" He had. And he asked if I would be interested. It was not an ecstatically enthusiastic invitation, but he was in a spot. Of course I was interested. Delighted, in fact. In those days anyone who mentioned the possibility of a drive to me was fabulous. I was engaged on the spot. He said, "I can't afford to pay you anything except your expenses, but we'll share any prize money." The deal was perfect as far as I was concerned.

'Metcalfe arranged that he would drive the Bentley to Spa. I went there in my own car, and arrived in time for the first day's practice and the scrutineering. There was no sign of Metcalfe or the Bentley. I told the organiser, "I'm sure he's coming . . ." That's all right, I was told. Next day there was still no sign of Metcalfe. I waited and waited while practice went on. Finally in the evening he telephoned – from Brussels. The Bentley's clutch had packed up there. He was having a clutch flown out to Spa. He thought he could get the car to the circuit and then we would have the new clutch fitted. Off I went to see the organiser again. He said reasonably, "This does present a bit of a problem because neither of you has driven here before. I'm not sure we can allow you to start unless you practice."

'The clutch arrived. The car arrived. There were only Metcalfe and myself to do the job – there were no mechanics in *our* team. The race started at 4 pm. All the previous night, and all the morning of the day of the race, we worked on this monster of a Bentley, stripping down the gearbox, removing the clutch and fitting the new one. We eventually towed the car down to the track, and when the race started we were still buttoning up the last few nuts and bolts. Metcalfe started about five minutes after the others. I'd never even sat in the Bentley, and neither of us had driven it round the circuit. I had thought, in view of the organiser's doubts, that we might not be allowed to start, but the racing authorities then were much more lenient than now. These days they wouldn't have let us near the grid.

'It was a terrible day. It was hissing with rain. And the Bentley was a bloody great monster on that very fast circuit, eight and three-quarter miles circling through the Ardennes Forest. Ian was due to stop after three hours, and at that point he was sixteenth in a field of thirty, which was pretty good considering that late start. I was standing on the pit counter ready to take over when he came in. A few moments before, an Aston Martin had come into its pit. The driver who took over was called Stallybrass. He had been in a terribly nervous state. He had said to me, "Oh Christ, I'm scared stiff about this bloody motor race." "But why?" I asked. "Take it easy." He really was jumpy. He leaped into the Aston and off he went like a bat out of hell. He got half way round his first lap. And then . . . It was the first time that I had heard an accident over the loudspeakers. The commentator was saying. "Here comes the Aston Martin which has just changed drivers, and it's now Stallybrass at the wheel . . . My God! He's going to . . . Oh, God . . ." And then there was a shattering crash and bang. The car went end over end into a field and Stallybrass was killed. And I heard this thirty seconds before I was due to take off in the enormous 8-litre Bentley which I'd never even sat in before. I didn't even know how to change gear in it.

'Metcalfe came in and said, "Take it easy, Lance, it's very slippery out there. Bloody slippery." I went off, not feeling very happy at all. For the first half hour I drove very cautiously. I thought there was no point in any heroics here. And then I began to feel a little more comfortable. I was finding out about the gear change. It was a right-hand gate change, and I got the feel of it. In fact I *did* know Bentleys because I had driven the old 4½-litre Bentleys at Chipstead Motors. We used to buy quite a lot of them. So the gear change didn't present too great a problem. Anyway, I was settling down and thinking, it's rather a nice old thing, this car. And then suddenly the rain stopped. The leaden sky began to lighten, and in a little while the sun came out. And with that I thought "I am in a motor race. Let's get cracking, for God's sake. I'm just dawdling round here." So I began to go a bit faster. I started pushing the old thing round the corners, and I thought, "It's a lovely old dear. Marvellous." It was like driving a battleship, it was so slow. And everything it did was ladylike. When you went fast into a corner, it just slowly and majestically came round. It was lovely. I grew more and more used to it. And I felt, Christ! this is tremendous fun. And I started to use the power coming out of the corners in second gear. The power was fantastic. Put your foot down in second coming out of a hairpin bend, and the thing took off.

'After I had been going for, I suppose, two hours – I was due to drive for three – I saw a car coming up behind me, a blue car. I pulled over to let it go past just before a hairpin. As he went by I saw it was a French driver, Louveau (he killed himself eventually), who was leading the race in a Delage. Coming out of the corner, I thought that just for fun I'd use the acceleration – by this time the track was dry – to see just how much faster he was than me on acceleration. So I went after him and I thought, "Christ! He's no faster at all. I can hold him." I followed him through a couple of corners, and then we came to the straight, and I sat behind him. I could see him looking in his mirror every now and again, and there I was, sitting behind him. I followed him like that around the circuit, and I thought, "Fabulous. The old thing's going like a bomb." And it was. The brakes were a bit dodgy. I don't know what we were doing, but the Bentley had a top speed of about 160 mph. I'd been told not go above 3,200 revs a minute, ridiculously slow. I followed Louveau round for two laps, and then I felt, well what the hell! So when I came to the straight again, I thought, "Just for fun. I'll pass him." I knew that I was lifting off, easing my foot off the accelerator, down the straight. He was doing around 135 mph, and I knew that I had more power than that. So I overtook him. He re-passed me fairly quickly because he was faster through the corners than I was with the huge Bentley. Then I was called into the pits and Metcalfe took over again. After twelve or thirteen hours the new clutch we had sweated to fit packed up and we had to retire.

'An Aston Martin won the race, and afterwards their

manager came up to me and said, "Both our drivers have seen you out on the circuit in that enormous Bentley, and they say you were very fast. We are going to start a team next year. Would you be interested in being considered as one of the drivers?" Of course I would. To me, this was a fantastic offer. He said, "We'll contact you at the beginning of the spring. We'll be trying out new drivers, and we'll see if you're any good."

'I went away from Spa very happy. . . .'

*   *   *

In the spring Aston Martin gave Lance Macklin a try-out at Silverstone. He was asked to join the team.

'I was exhilarated. But I thought of my father, who had died soon after the war. How disapproving he would have been if he had known that I was signed up to race, even for a famous marque.

'I went to Le Mans as the spare driver that year, 1949. I practised, but wasn't given a drive. During the race one of our drivers, Pierre Marechal, was killed at White House corner. That meant that there was a vacant place in the team, and I moved into it.

'We went to the 24-hour race at Spa next, and I was in the team consisting of three cars, prototypes of the DB2 saloons. We did very well. A Ferrari just won the race. Leslie Johnson with the $2\frac{1}{2}$-litre Aston was second, and I was third with the 2-litre four-cylinder-engined car.

'A Belgian girl I had met ski-ing was staying at Spa, and came to the race. I rather fancied her. She'd read that I was driving. Aston's had asked me if I'd care to drive one of the cars back to England, after the race and I'd said yes. The girl – it's strange, but I can't even remember her name now – found me and asked me what my plans were. I said that I was in no particular hurry to get back to England. At which she said, "Come and stay at my parents' home." I told her it was a lovely idea. She gave me the address and went off. I drove up to her place next day, somewhere in the north of Belgium. That night her parents went to bed fairly early. "Can I come and say good night to you?" I asked her. "No. I think it would be better not to, because my parents' room is right next to mine. But if I can slip out, I'll come to your room and . . ." she paused for a moment . . . "say good night to you." That was fine by me. So I went to bed happily. About three-quarters of an hour later I heard the stairs creaking. The door opened stealthily and she came into the room.

'She got into bed – and a moment later we heard the stairs creak. "My God, it's Mother!" the girl breathed. She bounded out of bed and managed to get behind a curtain as Mother came in. It was like a scene from a French farce. I pretended to be asleep. Mother switched on the light. She looked in the cupboards. And then she went to the curtains – and there, of course, was her little daughter. In a voice of thunder Mother said, "Go back to *your* bed, my girl." To me she said not a word. It was rather embarrassing. Next morning I decided that this was probably no longer a good place to be, so I thanked Mother for her hospitality and drove off. It was very frustrating.'

Macklin drove for Aston Martin in many sports car races, 'fairly successfully, I think,' he says.

'When I first started driving for them I was introduced to an Italian, Prince Raimondo Lanza, in Monaco at the time of the Monte Carlo Rally. He was full of fun and very wealthy, and he lived in Sicily. "Ah, Lance Macklin," he said, "we are going to run the Targa Florio again for the first time since the war, and I'm trying to get people to come and drive in the race. Do you think you could get an Aston Martin and enter?" I promised to try. He offered reasonable starting money and he added, "You won't have any expenses because when you arrive in Palermo you will be my guest and stay in my home."

'Astons agreed. I arrived in Sicily on the night ship and I was told that the car could not be taken off until several hours later in the afternoon. So I got into a droshky, a horse-drawn carriage and handed the driver a piece of paper with the Prince's address. That was all I had, a piece of paper with Villa Trabia, Palermo, written on it. We drove to an enormous wall stretching as far as I could see, with a pair of massive gates. This was the Prince's estate, about the size of Hyde Park, set incredibly in the centre of Palermo. The droshky driver said that this was as far as he was going. The last time he had gone into the grounds there were lunatics hurtling around in racing cars, and he wasn't going to risk his life, or his horse's, or, for

53

that matter, his droshky, in there again. I persuaded him otherwise and we drove at least half a mile to the villa. On the way
we passed the Prince's own little racing circuit.

'Sicily at that time was in the grip of a notorious bandit
named Guiliano. There had, in fact, been much speculation
about whether the Targa could be run because of his gang. But
Prince Raimondo Lanza got in touch with him – I am convinced he must have paid some tribute – and Guiliano gave an
assurance that the racing cars would not be touched. Guiliano
claimed to be a great racing enthusiast.

'But on the first day's practice the driver of a yellow Belgian
coupé came back shocked and furious. His car had been
fired on, and there were the bullet holes in the body to prove
it. Prince Raimondo sprang into action. He contacted Guiliano
with some indignation. The bandit apologised profusely. He
explained that the car was a saloon, and he and his men had
thought that racing cars were open machines. Furthermore it
was yellow, and that was the colour of the police cars. Such a
terrible mistake would not happen again. Nor did it.

'I started one minute behind the great Alberto Ascari in a
Ferrari. The race was run on a mountainous road that wound
all round Sicily through some very wild country. It was dark
when we started at about two o'clock in the morning. After
about an hour I saw the rear lights of a car ahead. I thought
with satisfaction, I'm catching somebody up. I got close
enough to see the number on its back, and I suddenly realised
that it was Ascari I had caught. I thought, "Christ, I must be
going jolly fast!" I was pleased with myself because the
conditions were horrible, very wet, very slippery, very dark. I
thought, "Having caught him up, I'm now one minute in front
of him, and he is one of the favourites in the race. All I've got
to do is sit behind him. I can't go wrong." You see, it is much
easier to follow a car than to lead the way, and he knew the
road much better than I did.

'So I sat behind him. We were going up a mountain, a
winding pass, full of hairpins. Just before a corner Ascari overtook a little souped-up Fiat. Of course, he overtook at that
point so that I couldn't get past. The Fiat baulked me for the
next half a dozen hairpins – wouldn't let me pass. And this
allowed Ascari to pull away. By the time we reached the top

54

of the mountain I was able to edge past the Fiat, and I thought I had better get cracking to catch Ascari again.

'I was now descending the mountain very fast. It was still very wet and slippery. The road had straightened, but the light was now that strange murky cross between night and day, very tricky and deceptive. This was probably the main reason why I made a mistake. I saw that the road was straight, and below there was what looked like a fast right-hand bend, and then I could see the road in the distance going back up the mountain on the other side. I thought, "Well, this is all right, it's all very fast." And I went howling into the corner at around ninety miles an hour, and as I came into it, I suddenly realised that I had made a mistake. The bloody corner tightened right up on itself, and there was a ravine waiting for us to fall into. Oh Jesus, an accident! There was no hope of getting round the corner, and I thought the only thing to do was to aim the car straight off the road.

'We dropped a great distance it seemed, and then there was a terrible crash.

'I had thought it was better to go straight over rather than sideways and rolling down. As it was, we went straight down, bounced a couple of times, and ended up nearly three hundred feet off the road.

'I was knocked out. My co-driver, John Gordon, the man who had sold me the Maserati, was slumped beside me. I came to suddenly. It took me a little while to realise what had happened. I could feel something wet running down the back of my head. Something wet. Blood? And then the smell came through to me. Jesus, petrol! We were almost upside down, and the petrol was pouring out of the tank and all over me. That brought me back to full consciousness very quickly. I had a job to get out, and a worse job to get John out – a bloody great big fellow he was. But I managed it, and he came to quickly enough.

'The incredible thing was that we had stopped in a great concrete drainage ditch which had been carved right the way down along the mountain. It was about four feet deep and six feet wide. It had been dug to catch boulders falling down. Below it was a sheer drop of 100 feet to a railway cutting going through into a tunnel. If we hadn't got caught, as though we were a giant rock, that would have been it. We were very lucky.

'We climbed back on to the main road. A priest suddenly appeared from nowhere. He made signs and led us down a track and took us into a funny little house, and produced a drink and gave us a huge glass each. That perked us up a bit, and we walked back to the road. When the race had gone through, other cars came along, and we got a lift back to Palermo. The car was wrecked. That was the only racing accident I had in an Aston.'

Macklin tried to get Stirling Moss into the Aston Martin team. 'Stirling was driving occasionally for Jaguar. He wanted to get into a sports car team, so I took him to Aston's, and introduced him, and asked, "Would you be interested in having him?" They said they would like to talk to him. But, of course, Stirling's idea of money and Aston's idea of money were two very different things. They paid me £50 a year retainer and I received a share of the prize money. On my second visit to Le Mans with Aston's, I won the coveted Index of Performance award with George Abecassis and finished fifth overall. It was worth about £1,000 in prize money. We won the team prize in the Tourist Trophy at Silverstone. The year that I won the Index of Performance, I received a total of £150 from Aston's, having won all sorts of other things as well. And that included my retainer! Of course, they did pay my travelling expenses.

'Anyway, I took Stirling to Aston's, and he talked to John Wyer, who was then team manager. After about half an hour Stirling came out rather red in the face. "Did you sign up?" I asked. He said, "No. Mean bloody lot, that. They hardly offered me anything except . . ." His voice carried an incredulous note, as if he could hardly believe what he was saying . . . "They offered me *fifty quid* a year." I said, "Well, that's what they pay me." He gave me a withering look. "Well," he said, weighing his words, "you must be bloody stupid."

'Stirling had just won the Tourist Trophy race in Tommy Wisdom's Jaguar, and William Lyons, the Jaguar chief, wrote out a cheque for £1,000 after the race and handed it to him as a present. So he wasn't too impressed by Aston's fifty quid. Of course, Aston Martin's attitude was, "If you don't like

56

driving for the team, there are hundreds of other young fellows who would be only too pleased to drive for nothing. You are honoured to be in the team, Let alone worry about how much money you make out of it."

'All the same, when the first post-war RAC Rally was held in 1951, Stirling thought it would be fun for us to do, and asked if I could get an Aston for it. Aston's agreed, and, what's more, fitted a special low axle ratio for us. Those who know the present-day RAC Rally, or have seen it on television, realise that it is one of the toughest events in the world, with special stages fought out through forests at high speed, often on iced-up tracks and in fog, bringing out the best in some of the world's finest drivers – and with strict time controls everywhere. It wasn't a bit like that in those days.

'We started off somewhere up on the East Coast, and our first control was down at Eastbourne, if I remember correctly, and we had only to average 30 mph between controls. There were no forest, or indeed any other stages, and it was before there was any speed limit on the open roads. I'm not sure now how far it was, but say 210 miles. At 30 mph it gave us seven hours to do the distance. We arrived four hours early. (Modern rally crews will burst into hysterical laughter.) The question was what were we going to do with so much time to waste before going into the control? Driving along the sea-front, we saw a sign that said "Tea Dance". In we went, and soon we picked up a couple of girls and got chatting to them. "What are you doing?" they asked. "We're on a rally," I said. "What's that? Sounds interesting." Stirling said, "We drive around the countryside from one place to another. It's great fun." We looked at each other, having had the same idea at that moment, then I said to the girls, "Why don't you come with us?" And they twittered, "Oh, yes. It sounds lovely!" So off we went to the car park. But when they saw the Aston Martin with its rally gear and numbers they got a bit scared. They came down to the control with us, but when they realised that we were off to Wales or wherever they decided that discretion really was the better part and fled. Nowadays, of course, to be found carrying someone who was not an accredited member of the crew would mean exclusion from the rally.

'Off we went to the next place, and there too, we had so

57

much time to spare that we took a hotel room, got the hall porter to give us a call in five hours, went to bed, then showered, strolled down to the control and went off again. It was all very leisurely and very boring.

'We began to have some trouble with the front near-side brake which kept locking-on. Neither Stirling nor I were very good passengers. When he was driving I thought he was going too fast; when I was driving he thought I was too quick.

'I was driving down a mountain road in Wales. It was dark, rainy and slippery. Stirling was sleeping. I came down the bottom of this hill and I thought the road went straight on. But suddenly, as I got there, I realised that it turned right. There was a road going straight on, but it was just an entrance into a farm. I hit the brakes to slow down for the corner, and the front wheels locked. I thought, "I don't think I'm going to make it if I try to get round the corner," so I took the "escape road". We went bucketing into the farmyard. I was turning quietly, hoping that Stirling wouldn't wake up, because he can be an irascible fellow, when there were squawks from chickens and outraged noises from the other animals, and he suddenly sat up. Looked around and said, "What the bloody hell are we doing here?" There was only one reply I could think of. "Are we wrong then? You're supposed to be navigating." There is no doubt that sometimes Stirling Moss's language can be downright bad.

'Again, coming down a mountain in Scotland at night, we had a touch of drama. The road was covered with snow. On the road going up the other side of the mountain you could see rows of tail-lights unmoving. Obviously the cars were stuck in the snow. As we came nearer we could follow what was happening. The car at the crest of the hill would be slowly and laboriously pushed over by the crew of the car behind. Then this, in its turn, would be shoved over the top by the crew of the car at its rear. So the crews were really slowly pushing each other up the hill. "What do you think we ought to do?" asked Stirling, since it went without saying that we didn't want to join that queue. "Let's see if we can pass them on the outside," I said. There wasn't much room, just a narrowish grass verge on the outside and then a nasty drop down into a valley. That didn't deter Stirling. We went haring up on the outside, with the car sideways on the snow much of the time, and Stirling driving magnificently. We went past all those people – and they didn't like it at all. They were awfully upset, shouting and hooting. They thought we should have waited our turn like everyone else. But it was, after all, supposed to be a rally, with people over-coming conditions, not being mastered by them. There was no earthly reason why we should have joined the queue.

'We really thought we would score in what were called manoeuvrability tests. You drive into marked-out spaces, turn, reverse into something else. All as quickly as you can and without touching the marker lines, you slalom round pylons, and so on. Driving clubs still hold manoeuvrability contests, but they would be laughed at in a modern rally. Detailed diagrams of these tests were given to us before the rally, so Aston's laid out replicas and we spent a whole afternoon practising them. We found that were were equally quick at them, so we tossed up to see who should do them in the rally.

'When we arrived at Torquay for the end of the rally with these tests as climax, we thought that we must be well set for winning the whole event. I watched Stirling do the tests. He did them fantastically quickly without putting a wheel wrong. I thought, "That's really brilliant. It could not have been done quicker or better."

'The places were to be announced next morning. We went off happily to bed. I was convinced that we must have won the rally. I couldn't see who could have beaten us. We had a special low axle ratio in our car which gave it much better acceleration than virtually any other. Next day we went to rally HQ and asked for the results. "We've got the first dozen, so far," we were told. We were not amongst them. So we asked, "Could you tell us where we finished?" They looked it up, and we were told, "Seventeenth." *Seventeenth*. We were told something to the effect that "On test number (whatever it was) you put your left front wheel across the line by two inches . . ." I'm sure that never happened.

'Stirling was furious. We'd spent three days and nights on the rally, and we believed that we had been fiddled out of a win, or at least a reasonable place. We believed that they didn't want it won by Stirling Moss and Lance Macklin in a works Aston

Martin. They wanted this first post-war rally won by Mr Every-
man in a Ford Zephyr or something like that, which is, I believe,
what happened.'

*   *   *

That was Macklin's only experience of a major rally. Let us
go back to racing, in fact to his drive with George Abecassis at
Le Mans. He says: 'In that race I was the fastest of the drivers
in the Aston Martin team, consistently quicker than anybody
else. Abecassis was impressed. The HWM team was starting
up. They'd got Stirling to drive for them, and through
Abecassis' recommendation, I became their No. 2 driver. It was
Formula Two racing at first, then Formula One – Grand Prix.

'I remember driving at Rheims in the French Grand Prix.
Stirling was driving one of the HWM cars, and I had the other.
People were laying bets on whether he or I would be faster. In
fact there wasn't much difference between us. Stirling was
always consistently faster than I was because he had a tremendous power of concentration. I could usually go as fast as he for
some time, but then I'd start to think, "Christ, there's nobody
in front of you, and there's nobody immediately behind you.
What's the point of keeping up this crazy speed all the time?"
So I'd start to relax a little. And suddenly I'd find that Stirling
had pulled out fifty yards from me. Next lap he'd pulled out
another fifty yards. And this would gradually build up. He was
a brilliant driver. Absolutely superb. He was very young at this
time, only 18 or 19. And he didn't know anything about the
world at all. I'd already lived on the Continent. I spoke French
fluently, and a bit of Italian. So I really taught Stirling quite a
lot...

'After Rheims, Stirling and I drove down to Bari in the south
of Italy in John Heath's Citroen. John sponsored, owned and
ran HWM. He put the money up. He and George Abecassis
owned HWM Motors, which explains why George's recommendation carried such weight. Heath lent us his Citroen, and
really it was a signal mark of favour, because he was very
particular about that car and who drove it. At Bari Stirling and
I met an astonishingly attractive little girl who was Miss Italian
Air Force. We chatted her up and had some fun without getting

60

very far. Italians are difficult girls to get into bed with. Always most difficult.

'The next race on our list was the Grand Prix at Naples, but it wasn't for a fortnight. So we arranged to spend a week in Capri. Miss Italian Air Force accepted our invitation to join us when we could let her know where we were staying. It was out of season at Capri, with not many people about. We looked around and couldn't see much going on. We kept trying to phone our Italian beauty, but couldn't contact her. Just by chance, Stirling picked up a magazine and came across a picture of Miss France. He said, lost in admiration, "Look at that! What a fantastic girl! What wouldn't I give to go out with a girl like that!" So I said, "I know her. She's the daughter of a policeman in Monte Carlo." He didn't know whether to believe me. "Are you joking?" I assured him I wasn't. "Well, would you introduce me to her?" Certainly. "We could probably go up to Monte Carlo and find her there now," I said.

'I asked John Heath if we could borrow his Citroen again, and he very generously agreed. We left him in Capri, and on the mainland picked up the Citroen from the garage where we'd left it and drove off. It's a long way from Naples to Monte Carlo through the twisting route we had to use, and we did it in a day. Unfortunately Miss France was away. Poor Stirling was disappointed. But I wasn't going to let him down if I could help it. Another girl friend of mine was in residence, and things turned out all right.

'A couple of days in Monte, and then we had to go back. We drove as quickly returning as he had going, and popped John's car back in its garage in Naples. As we walked away from the car, one of us turned for some reason and looked at it. Stirling, I think it was. He said, "Christ, look at those bloody tyres!" Tyres were pretty difficult to get hold of in those days, and John had just managed to get a brand-new set. We looked at the car. "Crikey!" I said. "Oh my God!" The two front tyres were bald. Absolutely, horrifyingly bald. We went back to the car. We jacked it up and switched the back and front wheels. The back pair weren't quite so bad – Citroens were a bit heavy on the front tyres anyway. We thought that with a bit of luck John might not notice. Of course he did, and he was very upset. He made us pay for the tyres. We didn't have all that much money at the time, too. HWM paid us £50 a race. But we had to pay our expenses out of that. And we got half the prize money. You could just about make a living at it, I didn't really worry too much about money because I enjoyed motor racing. If anybody was actually willing to pay me, so much the better. Up to then, I had been driving my Maserati in this type of racing, which I had to pay for. And if it broke down I had to pay for the repairs.

'I remember entering the Maserati for a race at Chimay, the Grand Prix des Frontières again, where I had driven the old Invicta. Louveau, the French driver whom I had overtaken in the Bentley down the Spa straight, had a similar Maserati. We were friends. He had a garage in Paris and I kept my car there. He had a splendid Italian mechanic who was excellent with Maseratis and kept mine tuned up. Louveau had a big truck which we used to carry our cars to and from races, sharing expenses. We were both due to race at Chimay, but the night before we were to leave, he rang up: "Lance, I'm sorry, but when we started my Maserati up this afternoon for a final test, the throttle jammed wide open and the engine went straight up to ten thousand revs, and flew apart. So I'm afraid I won't be going, and you'll have to make your own arrangements to get your car to the race."

'At that time I was staying at the Georges Cinque Hotel in Paris, one of the finest hotels in the world. My sister was married to a very wealthy American, and they had a suite there. With it went a maid's room at the very top of the hotel. But they didn't have a maid, so my sister offered the room to me with nothing to pay. I'd been staying at a cheap little place, so I thankfully accepted. I used to stroll in and out of the Georges Cinque with the air of a man who regularly broke the bank at Monte Carlo, and there I was – staying in the maid's room!

'I had a truck of my own, a huge ex-American Army GMC, which I kept round the back of the château which was the country home of my other brother-in-law, now the Duc de Caraman, about thirty miles out of Paris. I had to be at the scrutineering at Chimay the morning after Louveau's call, so I jumped into my car, drove to the château, and brought the truck back to Paris. I parked this ugly great American brute outside the elegant Georges Cinque, and went to bed in my little top room. Next morning I started out for Chimay with the Maserati in the truck. Everything seemed to be going reasonably, although I couldn't get the old thing to go too fast, and I began to worry just a little about whether I was going to make the deadline for scrutineering. Ten miles short of the Belgian frontier the truck gave a couple of hiccoughs and stopped. What the hell was I going to do? I hadn't got a mechanic with me, and anyway it was a very difficult job to get at the engine. You had to reach it from underneath.

'There were some farm houses down the road. I ran and knocked on the first door. A peasant face, stubbled, with deep-set eyes, a face that looked far from amiable, gazed at me. "Could somebody come and give me a hand to get a racing car out of that truck" – I pointed; the stubbled face followed my hand – "that has broken down there?" A racing car in a truck that had broken down. This was something strange to break the pattern of his routine. His face dissolved in a half-baffled grin. "Un moment, M'sieu," and he went to call more help. Eventually two or three farm-hands came along. We opened the truck, got the Maserati on the ramps and rolled it to the ground. I put my toolbox on the floor of the car, over the *carnet de passage*. I closed the truck doors and said, "I'll be back. Can you give me a push?" They shoved. The Maserati started straight away. And I drove off down the road in a Formula One racing car without number plates, lights, or anything else that one has on a road car.

'They couldn't have heard much like it at the frontier. The beast I was driving was roaring its head off as I dashed up. I thrust the *carnet* at the officials. I was like a man with hell at his heels. "Quick! Quick!" I urged. "I've got to get to Chimay to race!" Nobody can ever have arrived before at a frontier control in a Formula One car, snorting and ready to go. Before they knew what was happening they had given me back the *carnet* in a reflex of pure astonishment, and I roared off.

'I arrived just in time for scrutineering. And I was second in the race. Next day I got into the Maserati and drove back to the frontier. They had heard the race result and were friendly. I was waved through, without formality, as though it was the most natural thing in the world for anyone to drive a Formula

One car through the frontier. And then – there was my truck by the side of the road. Covered in flowers. The farm workers had heard on the radio that I had come second at Chimay, and they had decked the truck with masses of flowers picked from their gardens.'

Macklin stayed with HWM driving with Stirling Moss for a couple of years. Then Moss went off to make his own way with a young fellow called Ken Gregory as his manager, a partnership celebrated in racing. And Peter Collins joined the team as No. 2. to Macklin. Great names. Great days. Macklin sold his share of the budding firm of Chipstead Motors and went racing full-time. He was living in the South of France, a pretty hectic life when he was home. And he was just about making ends meet by racing. There were no great riches. Nothing like what can be earned by the top drivers now, even allowing for inflation, for most people in motor sport in those days. But there was much exuberance and fun. The life suited Macklin. 'If you were a racing driver of any standing, people would entertain you. You would constantly be invited to parties. Often one's hotel bill would be paid when one was racing; and usually one stayed at the best hotels.'

Lance was able to live amid the opulent surroundings of the Riviera because his younger sister, Mia, had married an American known picturesquely as the Purple-Hearted Jell-O heir. Lance explains: 'Mia was a beautiful girl, an Olympic skater. She got a couple of silver medals for Britain at the Garmisch Games before the war when Hitler was there. The American's grandfather had devised a jelly called, with stunning originality, Jell-O. He made an awful lot of money. The grandfather, that is. My brother-in-law inherited a couple of millions. He piloted a bomber plane during the war and was shot down and taken prisoner. He returned to a hero's welcome in the States. The Americans give their men a Purple Heart medal if they are wounded in combat. He had been hit by shrapnel in his leg. So he got the Purple Heart. He was considered generally a fine catch for any girl when he and my sister married. My mother had bought a villa at Roquebrune near Monte Carlo, but in the winter she used to go for long visits to Mia in California, and I would move into the villa. My mother also found the Riviera too hot in the summer and she spent a lot of time in England then. The villa was run by a housekeeper and a maid, and it was free for me and very handy because I could go back there after races and entertain my friends. We had great fun.

'But we were talking of HWM. My best win with them was the Daily Express International Trophy at Silverstone. The HWMs were never really fast enough to be competitive – unless other cars broke down in front of you. Luckily they were fairly reliable, so you could keep going. So one might be fifth or sixth at the start of a race and end up second or third. In sports-car racing I was becoming a bit fed-up with Aston Martin because of the pay.

'When I was in England I used to home in naturally to the Steering Wheel Club to see if there was anyone I knew around. At the end of one season I walked into the Club and there was a message asking me to ring someone I didn't know at a Bristol number. It turned out to be the Bristol Aircraft Corporation. They were producing a new car and proposed to race it in sports-car events. They wanted me to be their Number One driver – at £1,000 a year, plus starting money. This was more like it, compared to Aston's £50.

'I thought it was going to be a very small, very streamlined little 2-litre car. Instead, it turned out to be a large – certainly much too big for a 2-litre car – saloon with two fins on the back. A peculiar-looking thing. We promptly christened it the Pregnant Grasshopper. I did a lot of testing with it on the Brabazon runway at Bristol, a four-mile runway about 100 yards wide, very useful because you could get up to maximum speeds on it. And it was wide enough to allow one to do some tight turns and see how the Grasshopper handled. It didn't matter if one did spin the thing. So I got some idea of the handling. It was most peculiar, and I didn't like it.

'We went to Le Mans, this team of Bristol 450s, in 1953. I started off in the race, driving the first three hours, and I wasn't very happy for a moment of them. There was a very strong smell of petrol. I didn't know where it was coming from. I thought it was from the carburettors, but it was very strong in the cabin. I thought, I wouldn't like this thing to catch fire suddenly. It would be very nasty. I finished my first stint all right, and Graham Whitehead, my co-driver, took over. Off he went – but he didn't come round. It's terribly worrying when that happens. And then we heard that he'd had an accident on his first lap. After Mulsanne there's a very fast right-hand corner before you come into Indianapolis, the Esses. Graham was going full chat round this fast right-hand corner, doing something over 120 mph, when the car suddenly burst into flames and, as he was in the corner, the back wheels locked. The car spun and went backwards off the road at very high speed. Graham was thrown out. It was a very nasty accident, but he escaped with virtually no injuries. He was very shaken, of course. An hour and a half later Tommy Wisdom, driving another of our team cars, came full chat down the Mulsanne in the dark, and his car suddenly did the same thing – burst into flames. Tommy managed to steer it to the side of the road and he opened the door and baled out with the car still doing 130 mph. He was very lucky. The crankshafts had broken on the cars, and when this happened, with con rods presumably coming out of the side of the engine block, oil from the sump was dumped on to the exhaust pipes. There were six led out of the side of the engine, and then underneath it in a row and across the other side to get them away from the driver. The oil from the sumps was catching fire on the hot exhausts. I went to see Tommy in hospital. He looked as though he had gone ten rounds with Joe Louis. He was pretty badly burned.' (*Wisdom once told the author with whom he shared a car in the Monte Carlo Rally that the burns he received in that Le Mans were the worst experience of his life. Fits of profound depression, a consequence of the burns, almost defeated his will to live.*)

'He was lucky to survive. There weren't any flameproof overalls in those days,' says Macklin. 'I was very casual about my gear. I mostly wore short-sleeved shirts, a crash helmet – you had to wear one – and boxing boots. In fact I started the fashion of racing-drivers wearing boxing boots. I took to them because we used to originally wear plimsolls with rubber soles, moreover, and if you got oil on the pedals, which you usually did in a racing car, your feet would slip all over the place, so they were quite the wrong sort of thing to drive in. I decided that boxing boots would be best (you remember that I had done a lot of boxing at one time) because they are very narrow, they have very little sidepieces, and very often in a racing car you don't have much room between the pedals. Wearing boxing boots you weren't likely to get your foot caught between the accelerator and brake pedals. They have soft leather soles which don't slip.

'After the Le Mans burn-out we went to Rheims for the 12-hour sports-car race which started at 10 pm and finished at ten next morning. I was driving in the Formula One race which followed the 12-hour event, so I said to my co-driver, Graham Whitehead, "You start the race this time, and I'll go back to the hotel and try to get some sleep. And then I'll come out and do my stint." I also arranged with him that if by any chance something went wrong and he didn't finish his three hours, to telephone me so that I wouldn't have to go out to the circuit. So Graham started the race and he went round for about two hours. I was in bed when the phone rang. It was Graham. He said, "Don't bother, Lance. It's out." The car had broken down. It meant, at any rate, that I got a good night's sleep before the Grand Prix. The total of my driving for Bristol's was three hours at Le Mans, for which I got £1,000. After that I decided that it wasn't quite the car for me. I felt that my reputation was becoming involved, and I couldn't see any great future in it. So I decided to break with them.'

*   *   *

Where does one go back and say with certainty if this or that had not happened then the whole course of my life would have been different? We are so interwoven with each other and the world we live in is so complex that it is rarely possible to point to simple causes for the directions that our lives have taken and the things that have moulded us. This is even more true of great public events like the Le Mans tragedy of 1955. What we can do is to take hold of a few small strands which we can distinguish from an almost infinite number. And one such strand is the fact that Donald Healey asked Lance Macklin, following his withdrawal from the Bristol sports-car team, to drive an Auston-Healey in the 12-hour race at Sebring in Florida.

'Donald Healey is a charming person, and I got on very well

with him,' says Macklin. 'He had, you remember, driven Invictas for my father. The Sebring 12-hours was a very pleasant race to go into. And he paid his drivers well for what we did. Donald sent the Sebring car across by ship, and his team manager, Mort Goodall, and I sailed with it. We were going to drive it to Sebring from New York. A little windscreen was fitted on it, because there wasn't normally a windscreen, just a little racing screen, and it was given a makeshift hood, because this was April and it could be very cold in that part of America, the Eastern seaboard, at that time of the year.

'We set off from New York at five o'clock in the morning. I was driving. Donald had said not to do more than 3,000 revs a minute for the first 1,000 miles because the engine was brand new. Nowadays nobody would dream of driving a car all that way, or indeed any distance, to a world-class race, but people used to do it then. There were we doing a steady 3,000 rpm, about 70 mph, down the New Jersey turnpike, a super highway, six lanes in all directions, and not a thing except ourselves on it. It seemed very slow to me. After a while I did vaguely notice a car following behind us. In ten minutes it pulled up alongside and a siren wailed. A speed cop. He stopped at the side of the road. He emerged. A great, tall fellow. Neanderthal cop. He shambled up to the left side of the car – in the States the steering wheel is, of course, on the left, but in the Austin-Healey Mort Goodall was sitting in the passenger seat on that side. But we had the little hood up, and the cop couldn't see in very well. He said to Mort, "I'm going to book you for speeding. You were doing 70." All Mort said was "Really?" The cop said, "Yeah. Gimme your licence." So Mort handed out his driving licence. The cop looked at it, then shrugged. "Where you from?" Mort said, "England." The guardian of the sacred speed limit of the turnpike was not impressed. "Well, this is going to cost you fifty bucks," he growled. "I don't see that it's got anything to do with me," replied Mort. "Wadjer mean, it ain't nutt'n to do with you?" Mort said patiently, "Well, I'm just sitting here." The cop peered right into the car and saw that there was no steering on the left. So he came round to my side. It was beginning to penetrate that we were taking the mickey out of him. He didn't like it. He took two revolvers out of his holsters and pointed them both at me. He

68

said, "Step outside." I hesitated. Mort said, "Christ, Lance, you'd better get out. He's not joking." I didn't think he was. About a week earlier some fellow had been shot by a New York policeman for failing to stop at a traffic light. Shot in the back of the head. I had to sit in our cop's police car while he called up his headquarters. Finally we had to pay quite a lot, fifty dollars, on the spot.

'It was a hell of a long drive. About 3,000 miles. I was driving very carefully now, being very cautious, and we were getting a bit behind our schedule on our second day because of this bloody silly speed limit of fifty or fifty-five miles an hour. We were down in Georgia and we came to a long, long straight. You could see ten miles ahead. It was just a ribbon of road across scrubland. Occasionally there would be a Negro's shack by the side of the road. Nothing else. I said to Mort, "I think we can safely wind it up a bit here, don't you?" He agreed. So I wound the Austin-Healey up to 100 mph and cruised along at that. Eventually we saw a little township in the distance. Long before we got there I slowed right down to fifty, and we came down to thirty when we reached the place, and went slowly through it – one of those little hick towns with a main street going through and out the other side. Just as we were leaving it, I saw in the mirror a flashing light in the distance. "See what that is," I said to Mort. "Oh, my God, I think it's a cop." I hoped fervently that he wasn't after us. Anyway, we drove slowly away from the town as though nothing was happening. And then at length this police car arrived, sirens wailing. It drew alongside us, cut in, and stopped us. Out got an enormous fellow with a ten-gallon hat and a huge star with SHERIFF written on it. He said, "That sure is a little whizzer you got there. I've been doing more than 100 mph for the last twenty-five miles and I couldn't catch you." He ordered us to follow him, did a U-turn, and back we went down this twenty-five-mile stretch of straight road at a steady 45–50 mph, and arrived at the town we had left half an hour before.

'We drove down a couple of side streets to a red-brick building with a big American flag outside. This, I gathered, was the courthouse. Mort said with what I thought was a somewhat unwarranted detachment: "You'd better go in, Lance, and I'll stay out here."

'I walked into a large hall. At the far end was a desk at one side. A fellow in shirt sleeves was sitting with his feet on the desk, reading a comic magazine. The Sheriff walked up to him and said, "Judge . . ." The Judge put down his comic and said, "Yeah?" The Sheriff said, "Judge, I was doing 100 mph for twenty-five miles and I had a tough time trying to catch him." The Judge said incredulously, "*A hundred miles an hour!*" He turned to me: "What do you say to that?" I said, "I don't think I was doing 100 mph," but I thought I ought to concede something, and added generously, "but I might have been doing eighty." Quickly I went on, "We've only just arrived from Europe, and frankly, you know, there's no speed limit outside the towns in Europe." This, remember, was a long time ago. The Judge looked at me with a sort of pitying interest. "Didn't you see the signs saying 55?" I told him I thought they must be for trucks. "In Europe we have speed limits for trucks, not cars." The Judge was not impressed. He fine us 100 dollars, added, "If you hadn't been British and just arrived in this country I'd have put you in jail as well." Then he went back to his comic.

'So off we went, 150 dollars to the bad. There was another hefty fine before we got to Sebring. A couple of strips of rubber across the road somehow indicated your speed, and two cop cars were waiting hidden behind a board. Donald said, "Christ! I think I'll fly the car next time. It'll be cheaper than getting you to drive it."

'The race? We very nearly won it. A Lancia that was leading became sick on the last couple of laps and just managed to stagger across the finishing line ahead of us. So we had to be content with second place.

'I drove Austin-Healeys in many races. They were not particularly competitive. But Donald, as I have said, was generous, and we went to the attractive and interesting events like Nassau Speedweek in the Bahamas, and the Mille Miglia. I did quite well several times in the Mille Miglia, and one year I won my class.

'In that first race at Sebring a friend of mine who was driving a Porsche, had an accident with it. Afterwards he had to put the car on a trailer and drive it home to Houston, Texas, where he was an architect when he wasn't racing. He asked if I would

70

like to come along with him. I was going to Nassau for the Speedweek a couple of weeks later, and I'd met an attractive girl at Sebring. She came from Waco, which is not very far, by American standards, from Houston. So I thought it would be a good idea to go along with my friend. I could probably call the girl and meet her again. I stayed with him for a week, and one evening rang the girl up. "Why don't we meet for a drink?" Without a moment's hesitation she jumped into her car and drove a hundred miles to Houston just to go out to dinner.

'We became rather friendly and eventually asked her to come to Nassau where I was racing the following week. She wasn't sure about it, but said that she would have to ask her parents. Finally it was all right with them, and she agreed to join me there before the race. I went off to Nassau where Donald had booked rooms for us at the British Colonial Hotel, one of the largest there. My mechanic and I had adjoining rooms. Sydney Oakes who ran the hotel was a very good friend of mine. His father had been the victim in a famous murder case which made headlines all over the world. The killer was never found. Linda, my girl friend, had been given a room well away, on the sixth floor. I hadn't been to bed with her, but I had hopes when she came to Nassau. Sydney, a sympathetic character, agreed to switch the mechanic up to the sixth floor and install Linda next to me.

'I drove to the airport to meet her and was puzzled by the great crowds milling around. There were always calypso bands to meet planes, but now, in addition, there were all sorts of brass bands, and lots of gentlemen in top hats. So I asked someone what was going on, and he explained that it was a great occasion because they were expecting the millionth visitor from the States arriving on the plane I was meeting. "We don't know who it is yet, because we don't know who bought the millionth ticket," he said, "but whoever it is will be taken out and feted and given a great time." So of course the moment the door of her plane opened Linda was ushered out first, because she had the millionth ticket. I just had time to wave to her in the distance as she was whisked into the Mayor's Rolls-Royce and driven off to another hotel where a sumptuous suite had been reserved. I couldn't get near her for a while. I managed to make up for it later, though, sneaking out to her hotel.

71

'It was in Nassau about a year later that I was first married. No, that's wrong, because it wasn't really a marriage. I'd met a girl in California to whom I was much attracted. I was racing in Nassau again and asked her to come over. It's a lovely place. If you invite a girl to Nassau you're halfway there already.

'We were staying at a place called the Pilot House Club, and we were having a party one evening. Rosa, this American girl, was there with about ten other people. Somebody – I don't remember who – said, "Lance, why don't you get married?" I thought for a moment and said, "I don't know. There's no reason why I should – or shouldn't." And somebody else put in, "Why don't you marry Rosa? After all, you've been going around with her for the last five months. It would be a good idea." And Donald Healey agreed. He said, "I'll tell you what – if you get married to Rosa, I'll give the party!" Everybody said, "What a fabulous idea! We'll have a great big party!"

'I'd had a few drinks and I was feeling very merry, and I thought, "Why not? It sounds like a good idea." You can get married pretty quickly in Nassau, about twenty-four hours, I believe. Rosa was quite happy about it. She had been married, but was divorced. So next morning we went to the town hall and filled in various forms. I had a British passport; I hadn't been married before; so there was no problem as far as I was concerned. But Rosa was American and had been married. So the authorities told her, "We'll have to check up with your lawyers to make sure you are divorced, and so on." And she said there was no problem, gave them the phone number and address of her lawyers in California so that they could be cabled. And the party was arranged for the following day. Since Healey was giving it, we invited a lot of people. The wedding was due to take place at 11 in the morning.

'At 9 am I got a call from the town hall. The Registrar, or whoever it was who dealt with marriages, said: "Mr Macklin, I'm afraid I've got a problem. Her lawyers have replied that your fiancée is not legally divorced since her husband never signed the final papers." Rosa couldn't believe it. I told the Registrar, "We'll come along at eleven o'clock and talk to you about it." Along we went. But they said they couldn't marry us. Donald was supposed to be the best man. He was a bit

Macklin's first race. The year:
1948. The event: the grandly-
titled Grand Prix des Frontières
at Chimay, Belgium. The car: a
veteran even then, an Invicta
built by his father. The car was
outclassed, but not Macklin.

A real racing car. Macklin comes
through the pits in the rain at Spa
in 1953. It isn't the finest day ever
for racing. Spa is one of the
world's most difficult tracks. The
weather doesn't help. But the
driver would not want to be doing
anything else.

Alfred Neubauer, the
Mercedes racing team
manager, talks to Pierre
Levegh. In 1952, moved by
Levegh's solo effort at
Le Mans, Neubauer had
promised him a drive the next
time Mercedes came back to
the 24-hour race. Levegh had
two years to wait . . .

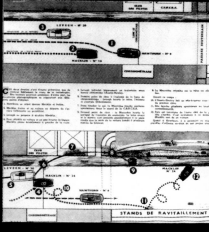

The diagrams reconstruct the sequence of
events in motor racing's greatest tragedy.
(above) Hawthorn pulls in front of Mack
to go into the pits. Then (below) it happen
Macklin pulls out to avoid Hawthorn. The
Austin-Healey is hit by Levegh's Merced
It hits (fig 8) the concrete side of the tunn
way and engine and front suspension hu
into the crowd. Macklin is sent spinning

A smoking heap of metal, almost unrecognisable as even remains of a car. But this is all that is left of Levegh's mighty Mercedes 300SLR, the pride of Stuttgart. The driver and 81 others died. The race goes on.

Minus a wheel, its back stoved in Macklin's Austin-Healey has been placed tidily out of the way. Miraculously the driver survived. And the race goes on.

They say Mass in the open on Sundays at Le Mans. But this priest has earlier work to do. He gives the last rites to a victim. The race goes on.

Where it happened . . . Macklin, in dark glasses, points out to Inquiry officials, incl. Judge Zadoc-Kahn, extreme right, what took place.

A shattering crash. . . a blinding gout of flame. . . panic-stricken spectators race frantically for safety

A votre santé, Monsieur Hawthorn Good health . . . the ironical headline in *L'Auto-Journal*, to this picture of Hawthorn raising champagne to his lips, with an arm round co-driver Ivor Bueb. They have just won the Le Mans 24-hour But 82 lives have been lost. Hardly a moment, *L'Auto-Journal* felt, for celebration.

upset. He said, "We've ordered this party now, and everybody's coming. I don't know what's the best thing to do." I had an inspiration. "Why don't we just say we got married? Nobody's going to know whether we did or we didn't. They're all expecting us to, so let's say we got married, and when we get back to the States after the race, we'll go to a local justice and get married there."

'We announced to everybody that we were married and had a marvellous party, but we never did manage to get to a local justice, and it was probably just as well, because after about six months I decided that it wasn't such a good idea. Rosa agreed and we separated, although she was with me at the time of the Le Mans disaster.

'There were few dull moments. Racing drivers in those days could have a hectic social life. They were not so subject to the pressures and discipline of today's enormously more commercialised racing with its never-ending and increasingly difficult search for sponsors who must get their money's worth in results.

'I remember that one year I met an American girl at a party at Le Mans. She was petite, dark-haired, with a nice figure, a very attractive little girl. She told me that she was in Europe for a month or so. I mentioned that I lived in the south of France, and she said that she was going there. I said, naturally, "Marvellous. Give me a ring." I thought no more about her.

'About a month later I was staying in Monte Carlo when the phone rang. "Lance, this, is Greta." Who the devil, I tried to remember, was Greta? She recalled the Le Mans party, and, what was more, said that she was only a few miles away in Nice. "Fine," I said, "We must get together." Indeed we must, she replied, but it had to be now, because next morning she was flying to Holland. "That's a pity," I said with genuine regret, "because I'm invited to a gala dinner this evening at the Summer Sporting Club." You see, I couldn't take her to the gala. It was a full-evening-dress affair, with special tables, six or eight people at each, and I'd been invited to somebody's table. Greta was disappointed, bitterly disappointed she said. She'd been looking forward so intensely to our meeting. I was not the man to disappoint a girl if I could help it, so I said, "Come over to Monte Carlo and we'll have a drink." I wasn't the man to miss a gala either, if I could help it. This one didn't start

73

until about 9.30. She took a taxi and we met in the Hôtel de Paris. What a pity, she said, looking meaningfully at me, that I had to go to that damned gala. There was a way round this difficulty, I told her. I suggested that Greta went to the Summer Cinema, an open-air affair in Monte Carlo, with the latest films. I took her there and told her, "This show finishes at 11.30. I'll be able to get away from the gala at midnight and I'll meet you then at the Tip Top Club." This is a famous night spot in Monte. Eventually I collected Greta there and we spent the night together. All very satisfactory.

'From that perfectly ordinary beginning I had the most terrible problems with that girl. She became quite mad, it seemed to me. She used to hound me. She followed me around month after month. She would stand outside the villa and call my name in the middle of the night. It was difficult, because by that time I had another girl friend. I tried explaining reasonably to Greta that it was all over. Nothing that I could say made any difference. And she had an uncanny way of knowing where I was, at what hotel I was staying, and she would suddenly turn up. I would groan, *"It's that bloody girl again!"* She made my life a misery for a couple of years. She followed me all over Europe. And when I raced in the States, sure enough, there she'd be. She would ring in the middle of the night.

'Not only was she an infernal nuisance, but I began to get worried because she wrote some very threatening letters saying that she was going to throw acid in my face or shoot me. It was the time that Ruth Ellis shot dead her racing-driver boy friend David Blakely. Greta, charming little girl, used to write, "You see what happened to David Blakely. That's what's going to happen to you." In the end I got so fed up that when I was in New York I went to the police, told a detective what was happening, and showed him the letters. He said, "Leave it to me. We'll call her in and frighten her off." He must have done, because I never heard another word from her. A doctor friend to whom I showed the letters told me it often happened with men at all in the public eye – girls get a fixation about them. It can be very serious. It was almost enough to put me off women. Almost.'

*   *   *

Of course it was inevitable that in the narrow circle of top racing drivers Lance Macklin and Mike Hawthorn should encounter each other off the track as well as on it.

'I first met Mike,' says Macklin, 'soon after he started racing. He was driving a Cooper-Bristol. He came into Formula Two, and I always got on with him. I always thought that as a driver he was brilliant on some days, but not all that consistent. Some days he was almost second class; he wouldn't be all that fast, usually because he had a hangover from a party the night before. People used to say to me, "I think that Mike Hawthorn's better than Stirling Moss, don't you?" I would say that Mike Hawthorn on his best day was as good as Stirling on his average day.

'He was an amusing character. A practical joker. And he was always one for big parties after races. And he had an eye – we all had – for the girls. I remember the year he won the French Grand Prix at Rheims. It was a fabulous race. He was neck and neck with Fangio all the way. I saw them both at close quarters – I was driving an HWM.

'After the race Mike said to me, "What are you doing tonight?" For once I wasn't doing anything in particular. Said Mike, "I've got a date with a little girl who is very attractive. But her parents will only allow her out if her sister comes too. The sister is rather nice. Perhaps you would like to come along and make up the four?" That was fine by me.

'We picked up the girls and decided not to go to a restaurant in Rheims, because if we saw anybody we knew, or, more to the point, if they saw us, it could have been rather tiresome. So we got into Mike's Ferrari and drove to a little town fifteen or twenty miles away, found a bistro and had dinner. We drove back to Rheims at about eleven o'clock, straight to the hotel where Mike and I were staying. Mike turned to me and said, "Look, Chantal" (*I'll call her that*) "and I are going up to my room. You can sit in the car and wait for us, or perhaps Janine" (*I'll call her that*) "would like to go up to your room." I said, "I think Janine had better come to my room, and we'll wait for you there." Janine was quite agreeable. She could have been only about seventeen, and really I was not baby-snatching, so what went on in my room was quite harmless. At about 2 am Mike knocked on my door and said that we'd better get the girls back, so we took them home. And that was that. We moved on to other places and other people.

'A few months later during the Paris Motor Show I was on the Aston Martin or perhaps the Rolls-Royce stand when a girl of about nineteen appeared and said, "Can I have a talk with you? I have something serious to tell you about." It was Chantal. I looked at her and said, "My Gawd! Yes."

'Chantal told me: "The problem is this. I'm pregnant and Mike Hawthorn is the father. I don't really mind about it. But my family know, and I've virtually been thrown out by my father." Chantal came from a well-to-do family. There was no question of an abortion at that time – and especially not in France. Those were far more difficult days for a girl in Chantal's situation than now.

She said, "The only thing I want is for Mike to recognise the child." In France if the child is recognised by the father then it can take his name and is not branded as illegitimate. But if the father refuses to recognise it, the child is classified as illegitimate. "It's only a formality," said Chantal. "I'm not asking Mike for anything at all. But I wonder, as you are a friend of his, if you could see him and tell him the position, and ask would he recognise the child? It would make things much easier for the child in future." I found that I was beginning to like little Chantal. I said that I would certainly talk to Mike.

'Soon afterwards I phoned Mike and told him and said, "Frankly, you know, I think you ought to do it, because it doesn't mean very much to you, and the girl is being very reasonable about it. She's not asking you for any money." What he said was, "Oh no, bugger that. I don't want anything to do with it. It's her own fault if she became pregnant. She should have been more careful."

'Chantal had a little boy. Next year at the Rheims Grand Prix it became an embarrassing joke because the girl was pushing a pram with her little blond baby up and down outside the hotel where Mike was staying.

'Five or six years ago I was in St Tropez in the summer, and a woman came up and said, "Aren't you Lance Macklin? Do you remember me? I'm Chantal. I'd like you to meet my son." The good-looking blond boy with her looked just like Mike.

'As a person Mike was rather a peculiar fellow. He could

be charming. He could also be unpleasant. He could be very hard in many ways.

'Peter Collins, now, Peter was different. To start with, I liked him very much. We were very good friends. We drove, as I have said, in the same team, and we had a lot of fun going around together all over Europe, from one race meeting to another.

'Once we were driving across France, and we stopped at a little hotel in the evening and asked for a double room. We took our bags up and looked around. There was a door leading out of the room into another double room. Peter looked in and said, "A pity there aren't a couple of attractive birds there." We went downstairs, and while we were having dinner a car drew up outside and in came a family, father, mother and two girls. Peter and I looked at each other. Interesting, we thought. In a few minutes the family appeared for dinner. The girls were rather attractive.

'Eventually Peter and I went up to our room and turned in, and we hadn't been in bed with the light out for more than ten minutes when through the side and underneath of the connecting door we saw the light come on in the adjoining double room, and heard feminine voices. Peter put his hand over his mouth, got out of bed, went over to the door and had a peep through the keyhole. He turned and whispered, "It's those two birds!" He spent the next few minutes at the keyhole, then he almost fell over backwards, and, trying to stifle a fit of laughter, beckoned to me. I jumped out of bed and put my eye to the keyhole. There, not a foot away, one of the girls was standing with her back to the door, bending down and taking off her stockings, revealing an expanse of backside.

'It would have been all right if we'd let it stay at that, but Peter, unfortunately, decided that it would be amusing if we opened the door and went into their room. The result was that they let out piercing screams, and dashed out naked down the corridor to their parents' room. Soon Father appeared. He got rather upset and cross and locked the door between our rooms. He was most annoyed, although Peter did his best to laugh it all off as a joke. Next morning when we went down to breakfast the family had gone, but word of what had happened seemed to have got around. The waiters burst out laughing

77

when we came in. And none of the other guests could keep a straight face.

'Peter Collins was a splendid racing driver. He was also a very nice, easy-going, light-hearted, amusing person.'

Driving in top-class company on circuits all over the world; parties; girl friends; an amusing, roistering life to counter-balance the risks he took on the track . . . that was Lance Macklin's existence until Le Mans, 1955.

Hawthorn

It was Lord Byron who said that after the publication of *Childe Harold* he awoke one morning to find himself famous. Something of the sort happened to a blond young giant of 6 ft 2 in. who went to the Goodwood motor-racing meeting on Easter Monday, 1952. He drove a Bristol-engined Cooper that had been tuned by his father. Few of the 50,000 crowd had heard of him. It was his first race in a real racing car. And it was also the Cooper-Bristol's first race.

The crowd buzzed when the 23 year-old newcomer, sporting a spotted blue bow tie, won the first of his three races. In the second one of the drivers was the World Champion, no less – the fabulous Juan Manuel Fangio. But the great Argentinian could manage only sixth place. First was the new boy. In his third race he sent the crowd wild with a great duel against another ace from the Argentine, Froilan Gonzales, who was driving a 4½-litre Ferrari. The Cooper-Bristol was only a 2-litre affair. It was the smallest car in the race. But Bow-tie finished second behind Gonzales. 'I dared not let up,' said Gonzales afterwards. 'Every time I looked behind that little silver car was there.'

All Britain knew his name after that. Mike Hawthorn had arrived.

He made his appearance in the world in Mexborough, Yorkshire, on April 10, 1929. His father, Leslie, an engineer, was imbued with the passion for speed and competition. He raced and tuned motor cycles, and, occasionally, motor cars. Mike was only a couple of years old when the family moved south to Farnham, Surrey, where Leslie took over a garage.

Like Lance Macklin, Mike Hawthorn as a youngster saw his first races at Brooklands. And he, too, became possessed by the great sport. The difference was that his father was delighted and did everything he could to help. The young Hawthorn tinkered his way through two or three old motor bikes. Then he became apprenticed to the Dennis lorry firm and he got his first new bike, a competition 350 cc BSA, with knobbly tyres and all. What's more, he started riding in trials and won the Novice Cup in his first event. He used to ride to work, but his parents thought this was dangerous, so he was given the use of a little Fiat from the garage, and in this, he said, he learned how to corner fast on two wheels.

Mike moved on to technical college with the idea (Father's) of becoming a motor engineer. He wasn't all that good. He wanted to be in the driving seat, not at the drawing board. Father was pretty tolerant about it. After all, he too, was fired with enthusiasm for motor sport. The decisive step was taken when together they went to a race meeting – at Goodwood, as it happened. There Leslie made up his mind. Mike would get his chance to be a racing driver.

He bought the boy an 1100 cc ex-works Riley Ulster Imp, a car distinguished for its handling and roadholding rather than its speed; Leslie also bought, for himself, a 1½-litre Riley TT Sprite. The idea was that father and son would compete in their own classes. Their first event – and Mike's first motoring competition – was the Brighton Speed Trials in 1950. Mike won his class. Leslie was second in his. In his first season of racing his Riley and at times his father's, in 1951, the young Hawthorn did so well, including winning the Leinster Trophy, that Leslie gave up racing and put all his efforts into furthering Mike's career.

The way ahead, Leslie thought, was to try to get Mike into Formula Two racing – 2-litre single-seaters. The opportunity came in an extraordinary way. Robert Chase, a family friend and motor-racing addict, chanced to read about a Bristol-engined car which the little Cooper concern, later to achieve world-wide fame, was building for Formula Two racing. Chase offered to buy one of these cars if Leslie would keep it in racing trim and Mike would drive it. Chase and the Hawthorns went to the Coopers' little workshop at Surbiton in Surrey – and found that they were choosy about whom they would permit to buy their cars. They had sold two to approved customers. They were building a third. Who was going to drive it if they sold it to Mr Chase? Mike Hawthorn. 'Ah,' said John Cooper. 'Yes, I've been watching him. All right, you can have it.'

And so to Goodwood and fame at Easter. After which it was established in the Hawthorn family that the way Mike was going to earn his living would be by racing motor cars. The polka-dotted bow tie became known wherever cars were raced. Mike had started out in his Riley wearing an ordinary long tie. But it kept flapping in his eyes, so he took to the bow. A driver with a tie of any sort would be an object of wonder at any circuit today when flameproof underwear and overalls are the wear of everyone in racing cars.

What sort of person was this Mike Hawthorn? Boisterous, roistering, with an eye, and more, for the girls. Happy at a bar with a pint in his hand and his friends around him. Much given to squirting soda siphons at the company. After a race at Turnberry, in Scotland, when the car he was driving, Tony Vandervell's Thin Wall, of hallowed memory, packed up having broken its rear axle casing, he recorded: 'We had a jolly good party that night, a real binge, and that made up for the race – I sort of drowned my sorrows.' Much later, David Piper, the brilliant sports-car and prototypes driver, recalled in the present author's book, *The Day I died:** 'The fun was there, ten years and more ago. I remember the first serious race I ever won, the Leinster Trophy, in Ireland. In that race, right from the outset, Don Beauman was thrown out of his car and killed. Mike Hawthorn was a great friend of Beauman and he was there. Before he went to the prize-giving, Hawthorn came up to me in the bar of the Grand Hotel, Wicklow. I'd never met him before. He was recovering from burns he'd got at Syracuse. He said, "The beer's on you tonight, David, because you've won the race. Anyone who wins the Leinster is going to do very well, because that was one of the first races I ever won. Well, David, I hope you have a lot more racing, but you're getting a bit thin on top. You need a bit of hair restorer." So he picked up a pint of stout from the bar and poured it over my

* Gentry Books, London, 1974.

head. That was the beginning of the evening. You can imagine what it developed into. . . .'

And there is this picture by his friend Les Leston: 'He was blond. The epitome of the crew-cut American boy, if you can say that about an Englishman. The Battle of Britain fighter-pilot type. A devil-may-care English sportsman, who loved his pint of beer with the lads, slapping everyone on the back, a real rugger-playing type – although I don't know if he did play rugger. A great extrovert character, very much larger than life. He was a great don't-give-a-damn sort of guy, the sort that doesn't exist very much in the sport today because it has become so over-professionalised. His was the atmosphere of the days before the war, the era of the millionaire sportsmen, the Whitney Straights and the Lee Guinnesses, the Count This and the Lord That who used to be able to afford to take part in motor racing. It was a rich playboy's pursuit – Prince Bira, and people like that. After the war Mike, with Stirling, became part of the new school. They may not have been rich guys, but they were enthusiasts, and somehow they managed to get themselves into racing cars. It was part of the aftermath of war. We had to do something exciting after the nasty stuff we'd been through. So one got into a motor car and raced, or climbed a mountain, or did something equally challenging. Hawthorn epitomised all this. Yes, he would have been a great Battle of Britain pilot. He was that kind of guy.'

*   *   *

The really big thing that happened to Mike Hawthorn was that the great Enzo Ferrari signed him to drive for what was then the world's finest team for the 1953 season. It was an accolade for the young Englishman who had been seriously racing for only a year. From a race at Monza, Hawthorn went to Modena, near the Maranello home of the Ferraris, to try out one of the Italian cars. It was a revelation to him. He then went round the twisty little circuit in his Cooper-Bristol – and crashed on a corner. In hospital, at first in Italy, and then in London, he had to have fluid drained from a lung as a result. But still Ferrari wanted him. And yet Hawthorn, elated as he was by the prospect, hesitated. He would have preferred a

British car. But he had to accept that there wasn't one capable of taking on the Ferraris or Maseratis, and so he signed.

Almost at once he was off to the Argentine to drive for the first time as a member of the Ferrari team. The season opened in Buenos Aires, and the Autodrome was packed to capacity. Thousands outside tried to get in as the sun flamed down and the temperature and tempers rose. Police tried to stop the hordes of gate-crashers. President Péron said that they were, as Argentinians, his children. 'Let them in,' he said. The police gave way. Fencing was torn down by the mob, and thousands poured in. They lined the sides of the circuit as the flag dropped and the race began. They kept edging further into the roadway as it went on, making it difficult for the drivers to see into the corners. They held out shirts which they snatched away as the cars hurtled past, as if this were a bullfight. The inevitable happened on lap 21. A boy ran across the track in front of Farina, who tried to avoid him. But Farina's Ferrari went into a slide, and then side-on into the crowd herded deep at the side of the road. People lay there dead or maimed and dying. In the panic, another little boy dashed on to the track – and was killed by the Cooper of the British driver Alan Brown. The race went on. Ambulances dashed to the spot along the track and the wrong way round. One hurtled into the crowd, killing two more. These unfortunates were put into the ambulance, which then went on its merry way to the victims of the Farina accident. The death toll was officially put at seventeen, but it seemed many more than that to those who were there. There was a further victim. A mounted policeman tried to drive the crowd back from the track with a whip. They pulled him down and kicked him to death.

The death of those people in the crowd was a sinister fore-shadowing of what was to come in a couple of years. . . .

But 1953 held better things for Mike Hawthorn – in particular, the French Grand Prix at Rheims. Those who saw it were convinced that they had witnessed one of the greatest and most exciting races in the history of motor sport. For lap after lap it became a Homeric struggle between two drivers: the British virtual newcomer, and the experienced, brilliant Argentinian, Juan Manuel Fangio. And yet for a while it had seemed that Enzo Ferrari might not let his cars even start

83

because of his anger at a penalty imposed for an involuntary infraction of a rule by a Ferrari sports car in an earlier race. But start they did, with the major opposition coming from a gaggle of Maseratis, led by Fangio.

Gonzales in a Maserati, took the lead from the start. The Ferrari drivers, Ascari, Villoresi and Hawthorn, in trying to catch him, seemed to be battling for position among themselves. Positions would change two or three times in one lap. The Rheims circuit consisted of main roads closed for the occasion. Sometimes three cars would be battling abreast at over 160 mph along what was an ordinary French road, a thought to make the stoutest-hearted driver feel at least a shade of apprehension. The Ferraris were evenly matched so that all they could do was slip-stream each other, getting in close to the man in front and being 'towed' in the vacuum thus created. The 'towed' driver could go more lightly on the throttle and still maintain his speed, and then hit the accelerator and use the added power to emerge and take the man in front – who would of course promptly try to do the same thing. The race was not quite at the halfway stage when Fangio and Farina – driving another Ferrari – caught up with the Ascari, Villoresi, Hawthorn bunch, and then the situation really became tense. A slight error by anyone could have meant disaster for everyone. 'Even so,' said Hawthorn, 'we usually managed a quick grin at each other when we passed.'

On the 29th lap Gonzales, who had started with his fuel tank only half-filled to help him to make the pace, had to go into his pit for petrol. This let in Fangio and Hawthorn. They left the rest and began the duel between themselves that went on astonishing and thrilling the crowd throughout the thirty-two laps to the finish. It did not, for a long time, occur to Hawthorn that he could win. He believed that the rest of the Ferrari team were merely allowing him to keep pressing Fangio, perhaps forcing the master into error, while they awaited the opportunity to go past and take the race. For all that, at one point Hawthorn went ahead and thought he had shaken Fangio off, but seconds later the Argentinian was back at his side. They would roar down the straight, using every last fraction of power, wheel to wheel and grinning at each other, with Hawthorn crouching in his cockpit to lessen wind resistance. So close were they that he could see Fangio's rev counter. At one corner Fangio braked more sharply than Hawthorn had anticipated. The result was a dent in Fangio's rear. Fangio simply ignored the minor shunt. There wasn't even a shaken fist. Another moment came when Fangio came sharply across as Hawthorn tried to pass, but wrote Hawthorn, 'I am sure it was unintentional.' The pair of them went past a slower car side by side, even though Hawthorn had to put his wheels on the grass. He didn't know what was happening behind him – the pit had stopped putting out signals, and the mechanics were beside themselves with excitement.

It wasn't until the last ten laps or so that it dawned on Hawthorn that he could win. And it wasn't until the last lap that he got his chance. Fangio hadn't, for some reason, dropped into first gear for the turn at Thillois. They went round wheel to wheel. And now everything hung on the timing of the change into first on the last corner. Hawthorn just made it and took the chequered flag with Fangio a bare second behind him. The *Autocar* report said: 'It was a battle which exhausted even the spectators with its duration and intensity.' And *The Motor*: 'I shall not attempt to describe the final laps. The whole thing was fantastic. The crowd was yelling. The commentators were screaming. Nobody paid much attention to the rest of the drivers at all and the drivers themselves slowed up to watch this staggering display.'

Hawthorn hardly thought about the drama at all. And when he did, drama was the last name he would have given it. He felt that the spectators must 'be bored just watching two cars passing and re-passing'. What did worry him was that shunt. But after the finish, as the two cars coasted along, a smiling Fangio gave him a friendly acknowledgment. Hawthorn was the first British driver to win this race since Segrave in '23.

The 1953 season confirmed Mike Hawthorn as one of the world's top drivers. But then he found himself the subject of bitter and sustained attack.

*　　　　*　　　　*

Those were the days when the young men of Britain were called up for a spell of National Service in the Forces. Some were fighting in the Korean war. Many, if not most of them resented conscription with its irksome, square-bashing, uniformed discipline tearing a two-year gap in their lives. Naturally enough. And their parents were often as unhappy. Therefore when a young man was hitting the headlines, living, it seemed, the life of Riley, driving motor cars around the world, and apparently immune from call-up, he presented a very easy target for those on the look-out for such things.

As a seventeen-year-old apprentice, Hawthorn, like most such, had been granted a call-up deferment. In 1952 when he left technical college and began to have his first successes with the Cooper-Bristol he asked for, and was given, a further deferment until the end of the year. Then he had his Modena crash, and when he left hospital he was told by the authorities that he would not be called up (he had asked to go into the RAF) until he had passed a new medical examination. And then he joined Ferrari and lived in Italy, although making forays to drive in England and visit his home.

The attack was launched in Parliament when Hawthorn was again racing with Ferrari in the Argentine at the beginning of 1954. The Parliamentary Secretary to the Ministry of Labour, told the Commons: 'Exemption from National Service is not granted to racing motorists.' In that case, demanded Mr Kenneth Thompson, the Conservative member for Walton, 'How is it that Mike Hawthorn is able to escape his responsibilities?' Mr Thompson then added with that special brand of unctuous indignation that seems to be peculiar to some MPs, that it would 'give very great offence to mothers of decent boys in this country when Mike Hawthorn is paraded as a national hero in the Press and on the radio'. To which Mr Watkinson replied: 'The difficulty in this and other cases of a similar kind is that the man has to be in this country for us to serve a call-up notice.'

This was a heaven-sent opportunity for some newspapers, always anxious to demonstrate their functions as watchdogs of the public interest. The *Daily Express* urged: 'Take this friendly tip: Come home, Mike! Don't wait for the Ministry. It's time you did your service. What about the RASC?' The *Daily Mirror* was more forthright. 'Why not come home, Mike? There is a reasonable chance that you can still go on seeing the world – in a British uniform.' But the *Daily Mirror* was determined to be fair. 'Nobody suggests', it went on, 'that Mr Hawthorn, a strapping six-footer of twenty-five, has dodged the column by remaining abroad so that the Ministry of Labour can't get at him. His duties and his inclinations have often brought him back to Britain. Only last month he could have been found at a Berkshire rally. In December he was in this country. Earlier the Ministry could have reached him at Silverstone or Goodwood. Did they try? . . . Or is there a hole in the Ministry's dragnet big enough to drive a Ferrari through? Thousands of conscripts in Germany, Korea and the Canal Zone will want to know the answers – TOOT SWEET !'

A couple of months later the House of Commons again occupied itself with the affairs of Mike Hawthorn. The question of his call-up was raised by Mr William Keenan, Labour member for Kirkdale, to show that this grave matter cut across Party barriers, assisted by his Conservative colleague, the indefatigable Mr Kenneth Thompson. Mr Harold (later Lord) Watkinson expressed the hope that 'Mike Hawthorn will do what I understand he said he proposes he will do and return to this country. I can assure the House that if he does return we shall be delighted to call him up very rapidly indeed.'

Hawthorn was less than cautious in replying. Interviewed in Modena, he was reported as saying: 'Surely walking around in uniform is an easy life compared to racing flat-out day after day?' He added reasonably: 'It is not that I am dodging my responsibilities. If the Ministry of Labour really wanted to call me up they could have done so months ago. It is not my fault that I am driving for Italy and not for Britain. I would jump at the chance of driving a British Grand Prix car. But we have not yet built one capable of challenging the Italians.'

But that 'walking around in uniform is easy' was the equivalent of an amateur boxer of undistinguished talent dropping what guard he had, and inviting a pro champ to hit him on the chin. The *Mirror's* famed Cassandra duly obliged: 'There's a young man by the name of Hawthorn – Mike Hawthorn – who drives racing motor cars very fast indeed. With superb co-ordination of hand and foot and eye he has become one of the finest drivers in the world. Yet, for all that, he is one of the clumsiest asses in Christendom. He has his foot severely jammed in his mouth. No, sir, "walking around in uniform", as you so contemptuously call it, is not an easy life. While you roar about enriching yourself and not bringing honour, as you think, to British sportsmanship, but discredit to yourself, thousands of other young men are doing hard, rigorous training.' And so on, ending with, 'Still we've got to admit that you have a nice turn of speed when it comes to getting off the mark from the Ministry of Labour.' And next day the *Daily Mirror* weighed in with yet another leading article: 'The case of Mike Hawthorn is not good enough. Here is a big-headed young man who thumbs his nose at his country. . . . The *Mirror* says: catch this DODGER. Unfortunately, he cannot be ordered back to this country. And he says he was not nabbed by the Ministry of Labour when he was last here. Right – then nab him the next time he returns . . . whip the skid-lid off his head and jam a tin-hat between his ears. Teach him to apply his talents to a spot of soldiering for the Queen.' But the *Mirror* perhaps wasn't on quite so popular a bandwagon as it thought. For, of the readers who bothered to voice their opinion to the newspaper, 66 per cent were *for* Hawthorn.

*   *   *

Amid all this hullabaloo Hawthorn had an astonishing escape from death on the track. It happened in the Syracuse Grand Prix in Sicily. He went into a corner close on the tail of the Argentinian Onofre Marimon, intending to try to pass him on the exit. Marimon, trying to stay in front, overdid it and slid. His wheels cut into straw bales which stood against low walls on both sides of the track. Hawthorn was blinded by clouds of dust and straw. He swerved and crashed into a wall. His fuel filler cap came open. Petrol poured over him and on to the exhaust. Hawthorn's car hurtled across the track and into the opposite wall. In seconds there was a pillar of flame 100 feet high. Somehow he got out with his clothes ablaze. He scrambled over the wall into a field and rolled around to put out the flames. Gonzales roared up – and thought that Hawthorn was still in his car. He stopped and ran across to see if he could pull him clear, ignoring the danger that the tank might explode. Then he spotted Hawthorn in the field. Turning, he saw that his own car had rolled into Hawthorn's and they were both ablaze.

Hawthorn had second degree burns on both legs, his left hand, wrist and elbow. In Rome skin from his back was grafted on to his legs.

After several weeks he felt recovered enough to ask Ferrari to let him drive at Le Mans. He was given a try-out at Monza. Ferrari, not without some misgiving, agreed that he should drive at Le Mans with Umberto Maglioli. They drove together to spend a couple of days in Paris first. And there Hawthorn heard terrible news. His father had been critically injured in a car crash. The Whitsun holiday was just over. All planes to England were fully booked by returning holidaymakers. On the last plane of the day a ticket-holder didn't turn up. Hawthorn was given the seat. He phoned to say that he would be home that evening. It was too late. Leslie Hawthorn had died a few minutes earlier.

Nobody really knew why it had happened. Mike Hawthorn sat in the coroner's court biting his fingers as he listened to what evidence there was. His fifty-one-year-old father had been to the Whit Monday Goodwood meeting. On the way home, in the dark and lashing rain. Leslie's Lancia seems to have gone fast into a corner, hit a bank, and somersaulted into another car. 'My father was an expert driver,' Mike told the court. An expert driver. A splendid mechanic who in the early days stayed up whole nights tuning his son's racing cars. A marvellous father, devoted to his son and the young man's career. A reliable man who would advise and guide selflessly. One who would always be there. And now would not be there.

The verdict was accidental death.

An hour or so before the funeral there was a knock at the Hawthorn front door. It was a policeman who had been sent at this moment with an elephantine lack of consideration to serve three summonses alleging dangerous driving six months earlier when Hawthorn's car had brushed – no more – a Post Office van. 'Couldn't you wait until my father was in his grave?' asked Hawthorn bitterly. He shut the door in the policeman's face. The man pushed the summonses through the letter-box and departed silently.

Even Cassandra was moved to write: 'I have no brief for Mike Hawthorn ... but I must say that the serving of a summons for driving offences against him just one hour before the funeral of his father was a piece of callous officialdom by the police. It was described as being "routine". *Routine? What oafish nonsense! Why not go the whole clumsy hog and serve it on the graveside?*'

In the event Hawthorn was fined £25 for trivial offences.

Tragedy or no tragedy, the call-up issue was still being plugged. The *Mirror* shrilled: 'Hawthorn HAS returned. Should the Ministry now act? Of course they should', adding with nauseating decorousness: 'Much as they must regret having to do so at such a time. It would be far better if Hawthorn presented himself at the Ministry instead of leaving the first move to them.' For whom it would be better, and why Hawthorn should present himself to the Ministry without waiting for call-up papers, the *Mirror* did not trouble to explain. For good measure it took a swipe at Peter Collins, who was also racing abroad. 'Some young racing motorists seem to be blinded by their own haloes,' said the *Mirror*. 'Otherwise how could they imagine that driving foreign cars in foreign parts helps their country more than soldiering for the Queen?'

The call-up papers arrived. Mike Hawthorn presented himself for medical examination. The doctors looked at his legs and decided it was pointless to continue. They asked him to report again in three months. And the position of the Queen hardly seemed to be menaced at all.

A few months later Hawthorn had a serious operation in London – for kidney trouble. And a month after *that* the astonishing Mr Harold (later Lord) Watkinson, Parliamentary Secretary and so on, told the Commons calmly and without a recorded blush, that the racing motorists Mike Hawthorn and Stirling Moss were not called up for military service 'because of complete physical unfitness before 1950'. Stirling Moss, in fact, also suffered from kidney trouble.

Convalescing after his operation, Mike Hawthorn began to take stock. A racing driver's life was, at best, chancy. With Ferrari he was paid solely out of starting and prize money. When he was injured there was no money – and there were medical expenses to pay. He felt that he ought to spend more time at the family garage which was his only guarantee of a regular living. Tony Vandervell wanted him to drive the Vanwall in Grands Prix – with a regular retainer. Stirling

Moss was lost to Jaguar, going over to Mercedes for sports-car events, so Jaguar also offered Hawthorn a retainer to drive in sports-car races. Ferrari was not very happy when Hawthorn decided to drive British. After all, he had made a sizable investment in Hawthorn, and for his part the Englishman was sorry to leave. He wrote: 'With Ferrari I had learned to think calmly and methodically while driving on the high side of 150 mph, I had learned to use some of the tricks with which the professional driver bluffs the opposition; and I had gained invaluable experience in coping with the hair-raising emergencies which are routine in racing, and even more in the testing which the public never sees. All this was priceless knowledge.'

None the less, Hawthorn had always wanted to drive British cars – and he had not served Ferrari badly. So he stood firm.

That was how he came to be driving a Jaguar in the Le Mans 24-Hour Endurance Race of 1955.

Levegh

About the turn of the century, an era that now seems as remote as the world's lost innocence, a young man from Alsace arrived in Paris, not short, it seems, of a franc or two, and with the will and ability to make more. His name was Veghle. It was the childhood phase of the motor car, and a captivating child it was, a romantic and perhaps somewhat mysterious child, with much promise of splendid things to come at maturity, the very symbol of progress in a world that, if not the best of all possible worlds, was manifestly getting better and better.

Veghle was duly captivated and, acquiring the means, became one of the pioneers of motor sport. He drove French Mors cars in the road races that were taking place all over the Continent. And he seems to have been pretty competent, winning several.

Some years after he retired, full of acclaim, his sister, Madame Bouillon, gave birth to a son, who was named Pierre. The boy grew up imbued with stories of his uncle's exploits. There was no doubt in his mind about what he wanted to do. He, too, was going to drive racing cars for France. That was important. Not just for himself, but for France. It was easier thought about than done. Nobody in a France just recovering from the terrible mauling of World War One, with racing cars and resources hard to come by, was taking any chances on young unknowns, whoever their uncles had been. Pierre got himself taken on at a garage. It was a beginning in, at any rate, some proximity to motors, and a chance to learn their mysteries.

Young Bouillon was among the hundred thousand and more

spectators at the historic first Le Mans 24-Hour Endurance Race in May 1923. It was won by the Frenchmen André Lagache and Rene Leonard. To the great crowd it was a splendid race, made sweeter for the patriotic by the French victory. To Pierre it was much more. He became obsessed by it. Possessed by it. A contest of skill, nerve and endurance between men in machines against other men in other machines, became more than a matter of sport. It became the projection of forces inside himself, of which perhaps not even he was consciously aware. Did the nephew feel that he would have to outshine the uncle? And perhaps fear that he could not? Was the test of Le Mans to him a test of something deeper and darker? The mystique of Le Mans for him makes an enigmatic and even shadowy figure of Pierre Bouillon.

He learned how to tune and tweak cars, how to induce them to perform far beyond the intentions of the makers. He began to acquire a reputation in such matters among enthusiasts. And he began to enter events himself. He displayed a fine control of his cars. He was a man who seemed to radiate confidence.

But he did a very revealing thing. He changed his name. He took his uncle's name, Veghle, and produced an anagram. Pierre Bouillon became Pierre Levegh. Jacques Ickx, who knew him, says: '*A man who is certain of himself, does not take the name, even in the form of an anagram, belonging to someone else.*'

Pierre Levegh was not among the greatest of drivers. He was able, and had a preference for long-distance events. He widened his interests. As well as the motor business, he became involved, and it seems inexplicably odd, in the manufacture of brushes. He didn't drive all that often competitively as compared with the real professionals. In sport, his range widened. He became an accomplished skater, an ice-hockey international, a first-class tennis player and yachtsman. He seems to have been akin to a thoroughly British type – the gentleman amateur, capable of occasional brilliance, but somehow never wholly involved. That, however, wasn't true of his feeling for Le Mans. For year after year he was there as a spectator. He got to know the circuit as intimately as it is possible to know it without driving on it. He studied the way the great drivers approached various sections; how they paced themselves; the whole business of driving the 24-hour race. And he never lost the conviction that one day *he* would drive Le Mans.

He had to wait until 1938 before he got a chance. The French Talbot firm's top designer, Antoine Lago, wanted someone to drive as No. 2 to Jean Trevoux, in one of the six works cars entered. Levegh's evident knowledge and air of assurance, plus the fact that he did have racing experience, moved Lago to offer him the drive. Trevoux had driven Le Mans three times and finished only once – a creditable seventh place. Who knows with what hope and anticipation Levegh was filled? What happened was that the car went out with mechanical failure before he even got a chance to drive.

There was no more racing at Le Mans for ten years. Hitler's men ravaged the place. They tore down the buildings. They used it as a fighter base. And Allied bombers hammered it. It wasn't until 1949 that it was put back into order and the 24-hours of Le Mans resumed its place in motoring history. That year Levegh drove in the Czech Grand Prix where he was fourth, but again he was merely a spectator at Le Mans. The next year he drove in seven major races, but still failed to get a drive at Le Mans. But in 1951 Talbot again gave him a place. It was not the fastest of the six Talbot works cars, but this did not matter too much to Levegh against the fact that at last he would be driving in the great race. He was forty-six and he had been waiting for this for twenty-eight years. With Rene Marchand as co-driver, he finished a highly satisfactory fourth.

And now Levegh was on fire with the desire to drive the 24-hours again. Fourth? He could do better than that. But he must prepare the car himself. He alone, he firmly believed, could prepare and tune a car to give him victory. Talbot insisted that their works cars must be works-prepared. Very well. He would still drive a Talbot, but it would be his own, prepared by himself. He bought a car, and he set to work. Levegh spent the equivalent of thousands of pounds of his own money. The engine was modified to the very nth degree of the limits allowed by the regulations. He gave the car a special lightweight body. He spent three times more than he could gain in prize money even if he won the race.

94

There was a record influx of more than a quarter of a million people for the 1952 Le Mans days before the race. *Autosport* complained bitterly that its chief photographer 'was being grossly overcharged' in one hotel. 'So many complaints were received', it reported with approval, 'that the gendarmes eventually sealed off the hotel till the proprietors agreed to modify their prices.'

Race day was brilliantly sunny. Charles Faroux, tall and upright at nearly 79, dropped the starting flag and the fifty-seven drivers sprinted to their cars. Nobody took any special notice of Pierre Levegh as he jumped into his Lago Talbot, No. 8, and roared away. The lap record went on only the second lap. André Simon, the French driver, took his Ferrari round in 4 min. 45.1 sec., knocking seven-tenths of a second off Moss's record of a year before. Just one lap later, Ascari's Ferrari made mincemeat of this with 4 min. 43.6 sec. – nearly 107 mph with the race only fifteen minutes under way!

The stresses of Le Mans began to show early. The Jaguars were having overheating problems. Ascari was having trouble with his clutch. The Ferrari mechanics set to work. Back in the race he was driving like a man possessed. He put in a tremendous lap of 4 min. 40·5 sec. But soon he had to retire. A French Gordini, driven by the Frenchman, Robert Manzon, set the crowd alight with an electrifying challenge to the leaders. After two hours Simon's Ferrari was in front followed by Manzon. Then came another Ferrari, a Cunningham, and two Mercedes, the second of which was shared by the euphonious-sounding team of Kling and Klenk. Behind this came Levegh. Simon could not hold Manzon who went into first place and began to build up a considerable lead. Kling went into second place. And Levegh began to increase his lap speeds. At nine o'clock, after five hours' racing, seventeen cars were in the dead-car park behind the pits. Manzon was leaving everybody – and into second place came Pierre Levegh. Two French cars driven by Frenchmen. The crowd was ecstatic.

Night brought its added strains. The world narrowed to a white strip of road. Lap followed lap with the straights, the corners, the gear changes succeeding each other in a monotonous hypnotic rhythm. Fatigue ate at the will.

Rene Marchand was ready to take over when Levegh came

into his pit for the third time. Levegh stopped him with a gesture. Not yet. He was not ready to hand over. It was his car It was his race. So – not yet, Marchand.

He roared into the darkness again. To the monotony and the fatigue. Monotony and fatigue? What were they? How could you feel monotony and fatigue when your whole life had been a preparation for just this?

The Gordini lapped him. Levegh was not seriously worried. The real threat came from the Mercedes. And he was two laps in front of their leading car. Midnight. The Gordini well ahead. The early hours brought a thick ground mist. The Gordini and the Levegh Talbot went round as though immune to any mortal peril. A short-circuit put the Kling-Klenk Mercedes out. It is said that Uhlenhaut, the Mercedes development engineer, chased the Bosch electrical firm's representative with a jack-handle. A splendid little cameo, unless you happened to be the Bosch representative.

A quarter to four in the morning and the Gordini developed brake trouble that ended its effort. The crowd – such as were awake – sighed, but were not unduly dejected. For now Levegh was well in the lead. Halfway through the race he was almost four laps ahead of the leading Mercedes, which was in second place, with another Mercedes laying third. And now the dominant trait in Levegh's make-up began to assert itself. The conflicting forces within him could never be decisively resolved. They produced, instead, an unyielding, unthinking obstinacy. Even he now began to feel the pressures of extreme weariness. In his pit his wife and the rest of the team willing him to come in, to have some respite, strained in the early light for a sight of their car. Again and again Levegh flashed past. All the people in the pit, even Madame Levegh, thought it. Some said it. Levegh's obstinacy was foolish. He must have some sleep, even if only for an hour or two. Marchand was perfectly able to maintain the position.

Car No. 8 went past. Not yet. Not yet.

In the Mercedes pit, Alfred Neubauer, the massive team manager, sat alert but unmoving. His two remaining cars were maintaining second and third positions without fuss or drama. He was satisfied for the situation to remain that way for the time being. Neubauer was a first-class strategist. There was no need yet for an attack on the Talbot's lead. And if things went on this way he did not think there would be a need. When he wanted his drivers to change they changed. That was how it should be. Four laps behind or not, Alfred Neubauer was not perturbed.

The sun came up and the day grew bright. Madame Levegh evolved a desperate and pathetic little subterfuge. When Pierre came in eventually all he would want for himself, she said, would be an orange. She would make an excuse to get him out of the car while she sliced the orange for him. Marchand would lurk out of the way, already helmeted and ready to go. As soon as Levegh was a couple of steps away from the car Marchand was to leap in and drive off. A couple of hours later he would come into the pits and Levegh, refreshed, would take over again. It was his his car, his race. Nobody disputed that. But – he must sleep.

Levegh came in for petrol. Madame Levegh, petite and dark-haired, tried her little orange trick. His face a grey mask, Levegh insisted that the orange be brought to him. In the car. Look, they told him, you're tired. We'll let you drive later. You *must* let Rene take over for a while. This time he did not even say 'Not yet'. What he did say was what they knew he had intended all along. 'I'm staying with her. I'm going to do it myself.'

He went off again to the rack of the Le Mans circuit, and, astonishingly, he was driving like an angel. Exhausted as he was, he was driving as he had never been able to do before. He was driving well above his own ability. The crowd was vibrant with his name. If nobody had noticed him at the start of the race an eternity ago, now he was almost a national hero. It was absurd, it was impossible, that this man in his Talbot should be leading the race by miles. Impossible. But it was happening. Past the pits again came car No. 8. Madame Levegh, Marchand, and the mechanics caught a glimpse of him, head to one side, chin down. They looked despairingly at each other. Pierre could not go on much longer. He was throwing away victory.

At mid-morning he came in to refuel. He was no longer a man. He was an automaton. He took a gulp of mineral water. And then he thought he was being drugged, and spat the water out. Marchand tried to get into the car. Levegh summoned up the strength to thrust him away, and then took off. Neubauer could see something of what was happening in the Levegh pit. His conclusion was that Levegh must crack if he stayed in his car. And he believed that the Frenchman would not leave his Talbot.

He was still driving superbly, that was the astonishing thing. Still in a wholly commanding lead. But it was driving by a whole series of conditioned reflexes. Straights, braking, gear changes, the lines for corners, he went through the actions like a puppet being twitched, but smoothly and precisely, unlike any other puppet anyone in the crowd had ever seen. So they did not know that he had become a puppet and they cheered and cheered Levegh. . . .

Four hours to go. Only nineteen cars were left in the race. And still Levegh was out in front on his own. And still the Mercedes were laps behind. There was only one more fuelling stop allowed. Levegh's face was turning from grey to green. His eyes burned deep under his brows. His face was set in a grimace because of stomach pain due to vertigo. He remained in the car. Marchand pulled at him and yelled. Madame Levegh spoke to him. The mechanics added their voices. A writer friend had gone to the pits. Levegh stared at him without a sign. It was clear that he did not recognise anybody. It was also clear that nothing would get him out of the car. The crowd cheered again as, fuelling completed, the Talbot took up the race again. Still Levegh was doing all the right things. Still he maintained his lead. But Madame Levegh wept.

Two hours to go. Levegh's head was lolling. But he was still way out in front. An hour and a half to go. But even the reflex actions were losing cohesion now. The Talbot had been averaging close on 100 mph. Levegh could afford to slow a little and still win by a good margin. His pit signalled him to ease off. He didn't read it. Or couldn't. At all events, he took no notice. An hour and a quarter to go. And then even the automaton failed.

In the last stages of exhaustion Levegh tried to change down from fourth gear into third. He got second – and blew up the engine.

Win Le Mans? *Not yet. Not yet.*

98

The Lang-Reiss Mercedes went on to win the race. Next was the second Mercedes of Helfrich and Niedermayer. An official car collected Levegh, more dead than alive, from somewhere between Arnage and White House. It brought him back to his his pit to an angry silence from the crowd. The stunned shock of Levegh's non-appearance had given way to resentment and hostility. The go-it-alone hero had become the man who had wantonly thrown away a French victory. The French never really forgave him. There was no gainsaying the verdict of Charles Faroux: 'The laws of sport are harsh and immutable. You have got to run all the way to win. We may be sorry for Levegh and his wonderful effort, but Mercedes met the essential requirements by driving a steady, well-controlled race from start to finish.' But neither Faroux nor anyone else knew the compulsion that had moved Levegh.

For two hours Levegh lay in his pit barely conscious. He did not hear the official results announced. But Neubauer came to him, Neubauer who was aware that in a sense he owed his triumph to Levegh. Neubauer said: 'The next time Mercedes comes to Le Mans you will drive one of our cars.'

*   *   *

Mercedes, deeply committed to producing a new Formula One car, did not return to Le Mans in 1953. Talbot offered Levegh a car. It was prepared by the works in the usual Talbot manner. Levegh accepted thankfully. He shared the car with the French driver, C. Pozzi. This time there were no go-it-alone heroics. There couldn't be. The regulations were changed to prevent him or anyone else attempting a repeat. The maximum spell of any driver was fixed at 80 consecutive laps and a total of 18 hours' driving. Several other changes have followed, incidentally. In 1956 the maximum became 72 consecutive laps, and no more than 14 hours' driving. A year later this was cut to 36 laps, but the total stayed at 14 hours. In 1958 the limit was 40 consecutive laps and 14 hours. In 1960 it was 52 laps. In 1961, 60 laps. The biggest change was in 1970, when it was laid down that drivers must spend no more than four consecutive hours at the wheel, with rests of at least one hour, and no more than 14 hours' driving in all.

But back to 1953. Levegh's was the only Talbot out of four to finish. The race was won by Rolt and Hamilton in a C-type Jaguar, with the Jaguar of Walker and Moss in second place. Levegh and Pozzi were eighth – ironically at a speed which would have meant a comfortable victory the year before. In '53 Levegh also drove in the Rheims 12-hour race in which he was unplaced; but with the French driver Philippe Etancelin he was third in the Casablanca 12-hours.

Mercedes stayed away from Le Mans in 1954, too. Again Talbot offered Levegh a car. For seven hours he and his co-driver, one L. Fayen, led the French entries, keeping the Talbot up among the first ten. Then the brakes failed. Levegh hit a bank near the scene of his 1952 tragedy. The car was wrecked. . . .

*   *   *

In 1955 the Mercedes came back, the magnificent 300SLRs. The Stuttgart concern was perhaps still a little edgy in the post-war world. They cast a very wide net for their drivers. They had the two greatest in the world in Fangio, the Argentinian, and Stirling Moss, the Englishman. They had the French André Simon, the American John Fitch, and a solitary German, Karl Kling. They asked the brilliant Belgian, Paul Frere, to make up the team. But they were too late. Frere had just signed to drive for Aston Martin. And then Alfred Neubauer recalled his promise to the Frenchman, Pierre Levegh, two years before. He asked Levegh to drive for Mercedes at Le Mans. It would be a marvellous public-relations exercise, too. The Frenchman who had so nearly won Le Mans on his own would now be driving for the German team which had secured victory only because his endurance had not been superhuman.

One can imagine the effect on Levegh. He was nudging fifty. It must have seemed to him that his chance of winning Le Mans had gone, lost in the twenty-third hour of the race in 1952. And now this. Another chance, a real chance, in the most competitive of cars. True, it was not a French car. But was he no less a Frenchman for driving a German car? A win by Levegh in a Mercedes would surely be as much of a victory for France as for Germany. All the old compulsion about Le Mans returned. He had thought that his moment had gone out there between Arnage and White House, although he had tried as few men had ever tried. And few men were offered such a second opportunity as had now come to him. Yes, yes, yes. Of course he would drive a Mercedes.

But the difference between the dream and stern reality began to manifest itself months before the race when Levegh began trying out the car. Artur Keser speaks bluntly of the situation: 'He was afraid of the car. In practice he was the slowest of all the drivers. And instead of admitting that he wasn't the man for a 300SLR, he insisted that he wanted to drive. He was torn between his fear and his ambition. Weeks before we got the reports that Levegh's lap times were – how shall I say it ?– inadequate, I asked Neubauer, "Why don't you get Manzon?" at that time the best French driver available. "I understand that it is very good for a public-relations standpoint to have a French driver. But Levegh is not the man." Neubauer and I were, in a sense, antagonists because we are quite different sorts of people. He was a great racing team manager, but – it is a difficult point to appreciate – he is Austrian, and Austrians have a very sentimental side. It was not a German logical, or even a British logical, reaction when in '52 he told Levegh, "Whenever we come back to Le Mans you will drive one of our cars." When I put it to him that he should replace Levegh, his reply was "No, no." '

Jacques Ickx says that Mercedes would have liked to have dropped Levegh, but would not go back on the promise. 'Levegh was going about with the face of a man in mortal terror. It was the stuff of Greek tragedy. His pride, his immense obstinacy, would not let him admit that the car was beyond his capacity, that he should step down. All the time Mercedes believed that he would ask to be released. Until then, having offered him the drive, they did not want to tell him that he was not up to it. So they waited for the resignation that never came.'

It was more than pride, it was more than mere obstinacy, that kept Pierre Levegh in the cockpit of his Mercedes. It was a compulsion, welling from deep inside himself, that he was, despite himself, unable to resist.

101

Disaster

So we come back to that Saturday afternoon of June 11, 1955. Back to the thrilling nose-to-tail, sometimes wheel-to-wheel duel of Hawthorn and Fangio, Jaguar and Mercedes, the duel that was providing those present with some of the greatest racing they had ever seen. It was almost 6.30 pm. Hawthorn is due for a refuelling stop. The signal telling him so has been showing from the Jaguar pit for two laps. Now, on the third, in accordance with standing instructions to the team, he must come in. He is closing on Macklin. Behind him, Kling has gone to the extreme right of the track ready to make his stop. Then comes Levegh, with Fangio behind him. Jacques Ickx says that Levegh has motioned to Fangio a mute desperate appeal – that has been understood and respected. It meant: Do not pass me *here*. Levegh did not wish to be lapped in front of the grandstands, before a French crowd, even by a team-mate. In fact his foot is hard down on the throttle to give the crowd a bravura display.

And now Lance Macklin takes up the story. It is the first time that he has told it in the twenty-one years since it happened.

'As I accelerated away from the Arnage hairpin, I glanced in the mirror, and then looked over my shoulder. When you are driving a car which isn't the fastest in the race, you want to know who's coming up so that you can give them room to pass. I saw a couple of silver cars and a green one going into the bend. Two Mercedes and, I presumed, Mike Hawthorn. I knew that I was going to be lapped for the second time by the race leaders.

'I snapped the gear lever into fourth and drifted my Austin-Healey through the White House bend at about 110 mph. In front of me lay the long, slightly uphill straight leading to the pits area, and beyond that a 130 mph right-hander under the Dunlop Bridge. My foot was hard down pressing the accelerator against the floorboards. The car picked up speed. I looked into the mirror again. A few hundred yards behind me, coming out of White House corner, a silver and a green car were neck and neck. I moved over to the right-hand side of the road to give them room to pass.

'I looked at the rev counter. I was pretty well on top speed – about 135 mph. The green Jaguar and the silver Mercedes were doing around 150. They were very close together and it was difficult to see which was going to pass first. It was surprising how long it took them to overhaul me.

'The Jaguar came alongside me. It was Hawthorn. I was delighted that he was clearly leading the race. I thought, Fabulous! Old Mike's doing a great job. At that sort of speed it is surprising how long it takes somebody to go past you. They don't go *z-o-o-m*! like that. They come up gradually alongside you, and then they're on their way again.

'By now we were approaching the dangerously narrow pit area at about 250 ft a second. Almost immediately Hawthorn overtook me I was surprised when he shot across to the right slap in front of me. I believed that he misjudged the speed of the Austin-Healey. It was known not to be a fast car, but it was going more quickly than he realised. For a moment I thought that he must be making way in case Fangio wanted to overtake him in front of the grandstand. In motor racing people often put on a display for the crowd, and I thought that Mike might be going to let Fangio go past to give the crowd a bit of excitement.

'Instead, I suddenly saw his brake lights come on twenty or thirty yards – no more – in front of me. I thought, Christ! What the hell is he doing? I had to stand on my brakes as hard as I could to try to avoid running into the back of him.

'And then I realised that I couldn't stop; that he was slowing faster than I was. The Jaguars had tremendously powerful double calliper power-assisted disc brakes. I just had ordinary little single-pad discs. At that sort of speed power

103

counts in brakes. At thirty or forty miles an hour it wouldn't make very much difference, but at 140 mph or so, the one with the most powerful brakes stops quickest. For a couple of agonising seconds I waited as the gap between my car and the Jaguar rapidly diminished. I hoped that Mike might see in his mirror that I was about to crash into him, and ease off his brakes. But I believe he was concentrating too hard on not overshooting his pit.

'I was as hard as it was possible to be on my brakes. One of the front wheels locked and I thought, "Oh Christ, I'm going to hit him!" I could really feel myself going into the back of him.

'In a last desperate effort to re-pass him, I pulled the car over to the left. It wasn't a swerve. You can't swerve at that speed without spinning or worse. I just managed to ease the car over enough so that I barely got past without touching him. For a moment I felt a flash of elation. Then the car went into a long slide, with all four wheels tobogganing. It was virtually out of control. There was a terrifying instant when I thought that my right front wing was going to touch the back of the Jaguar as I went by. If that happened, I knew only too well that I should be spun across the road – right in the path of the Mercedes cars behind us. But I got the thing corrected and pointing straight again with the speed at about 120 mph, although I still wasn't in real control. I was trying not to over-correct the slide, which is a danger that sometimes happens in one's anxiety in such situations. It would have meant the car swinging back the other way. I was acutely aware that there were at least two cars close behind, and I thought, "If I do spin, they'll clobber me."

'From then on things happened at tremendous speed. I remember them like a film indelibly imprinted on my mind.

'At the point where I got the car straightened out – there were tyre marks indicating the spot, and measurements were taken for the inquiry – there were 16 ft of road between the nearside of the Austin-Healey and the side of the track. I knew that, even though I was in the middle of the road as we entered the pits area, there was ample room for anyone to pass me on the left side of the road in the normal way.

'And then came an indescribable shock. I felt the most almighty BANG! There was a blast of searing heat from an exhaust near my face and my car was catapulted down the road backwards. Out of the corner of my eye I glimpsed a silver shape with the driver hunched over the wheel hurtling through the air ten or fifteen feet above me.

'Almost at the same moment there was a roar on my other side, and another Mercedes scraped by with only inches to spare between Hawthorn and myself.

'I could see the driver of the airborne Mercedes half hanging out as the car seemed to go on its side. We went along together for maybe fifty yards, and I could see him in the corner of my eye all the time. I didn't know who it was. I thought it was probably Fangio. A wheel of his Mercedes had gone within three inches of my shoulder.

'A kaleisdoscope of pictures revolved through my vision. I remember seeing the timekeepers' box going past sideways as I spun. I knew that my position was desperate. I managed to get the car more or less under control, in the direction in which I was supposed to be travelling, towards the Dunlop Bridge, but pointing backwards. I thought I had only one chance – to try to steer the car in reverse down the centre of the road for as long as possible by keeping one eye on the grandstand and the other on the pits, while braking hard.

'I hardly took in the tremendous explosion as the flying Mercedes hit the safety barrier.

'I managed to keep the Austin-Healey straight for a hundred yards, before it began to veer towards the pits.'

In some pits where guests were drinking champagne there was a rush for the doors as the Austin-Healey swung towards them. But the doors, you remember had been locked against those not invited to sample the hospitality. There were some broken limbs.

In the cockpit of the Austin-Healey, with the speed now at about 60 mph, Lance Macklin recalls, 'I hung on to the steering wheel and braced myself against the back of my seat and waited for the inevitable crash. You can't really steer a car going that fast in reverse. My head was nearly jolted from my shoulders by the force of the impact as the back of the car went into a pit counter. We didn't have belts or headrests. The car knocked over a gendarme and broke one of his legs. And then it hit a French journalist – both his legs were broken.

105

'A back wheel was torn off the Austin-Healey and flew into the air as I rebounded off the pits and careered back across the road. I ended up on the left-hand side of the track, blocking the fast lane, and with the front of the car facing the grandstands. Nine years as a racing driver, which includes many hair-raising experiences, teaches you to think coolly in a crisis. In the fraction of a second that it took me to assess the situation I realised that if I got out of the car on the driver's side it was highly likely that I would be hit by my own car if it were struck by the next car to come through. So I vaulted out over the covered-in passenger seat and then jumped up on to the protective earth barrier.'

It was a remarkably rapid and prodigious jump.

Macklin continues: 'My first reaction on reaching the protection of the barrier was one of relief. I was relieved to find myself in one piece and unhurt, and also that the burning Mercedes had ended on top of the protective barrier about 150 yards away from me, and had not gone into the densely packed crowd. I could see a body in the road. I thought it was the driver.'

Macklin then began to run towards the Mercedes and the body. . . .

*   *   *

Macklin did not know then what had really happened. Levegh coming up at tremendous speed found Macklin pulling over towards his path in order to avoid hitting Hawthorn. Stirling Moss crystallises the situation: 'If it had been somebody younger than Pierre Levegh, the result might have been different. It is not perhaps a fair thing to say, but somebody younger, somebody racing every weekend, or so, somebody more in the swim of it, might have had reflexes a little sharper.' But it was Pierre Levegh, fifty, who did not race every weekend. . . . His reflexes were sharp enough, says Fangio, for him to have thrown up a hand in warning, and this, says Fangio, saved his life. But they were not sharp enough for Levegh to use the width of the road remaining to him on the left to get through.

Levegh hit Macklin. The Mercedes went up over the Austin-

106

Healey and headed for the spot where the pedestrian tunnel emerges from under the track. The car struck a concrete upright at the side of the tunnel entrance. The enormous force of the impact tore the engine from the car together with the front wheels and suspension. They scythed into the crowd with devastating effect. The car went on to finish on top of the earth barrier.

Fangio, alerted by Levegh's upraised hand, saw a momentary gap opening up in front of him as Macklin's car swung round, between the Austin-Healey and the Hawthorn Jaguar. There was nothing wrong with his reflexes. With marvellous precision, he got through. That was the roar that Macklin had heard as he battled for control. And there were hardly inches to spare. Green paint from the Jaguar was found on the silver Mercedes. . . .

Flames reared high and there was a dense pall of smoke. Charles Faroux, in his eighties, stepped out on the track and tried to slow the race down. . . .

*   *   *

François Jardell somehow managed to miss his girl friend. She seemed to have vanished. He stood at the spot where he thought he had seen her. He saw the Mercedes flying, saw it hit, and heard an explosion. And then came a second explosion five or six seconds later. Jardell was signalling information from time to time about the state of the race to one of the pits. He wore a red sweater and a red cap so that he could easily be seen from a distance. But his trousers were white. He remembers vividly the woman who stood in front of him. 'She was a fat lady. She shielded me. She was killed. I think part of the engine hit her. But because of her I was not touched. My trousers were no longer white. They were quite red with the blood of this woman.'

Jardell did what he could to help the injured. 'It was awful. Many of those killed and injured had been standing on portable steps. They had cameras, and they all seemed to be wearing little eyeshades with advertising on them for Bonal, an aperitif. Since then I cannot drink Bonal. A man two or three steps in front of me was killed. The second explosion was just

107

like a mine. And this man was just like men I had seen killed by mines in the war. No marks of injuries. But exactly flat. But the most awful thing I saw was a man cradling a small child in his arms. The child looked as if he were dead. I could see he had terrible injuries anyway. But the man . . . the man didn't look as if he was seeing anything and his lips were smiling.

'There were cameras lying around everywhere. I'm sorry to say that I had a kind of awful reflex. In the Army during the war if we saw a camera around that belonged to a German we would take it, a sort of reparations, you see. So I had to suppress this reflex. I never saw so many cameras in my life. I saw a lot of people killed during the war, but suddenly to see all these people killed in the middle of a kermesse, a fair. . . . And the photographers were doing their job. Some were filming. And people were furious. They were fighting with the photographers, screaming at them, "What are you doing?" I heard one cameraman I knew, he was later killed in Hungary, saying, "Well, I'm just doing my job."

'But something I think much more important was the fact that ten minutes after the accident Mercedes mechanics were there and picking parts of the car from the ground. They went in among the people picking up bits and pieces of the Mercedes. It gives me the feeling that something was not right. . . .'

*   *   *

Standing on top of pit No. 3, Les Leston saw the Austin-Healey, which soon it would be his turn to drive, coming up the road from the White House. He says: 'Macklin obviously knew that he was about to be lapped, so he was keeping well over to his right, doing the proper thing. I could see the Jaguar and the Mercedes coming out of the White House corner, Hawthorn in the lead, the two of them going some 50 mph faster than Macklin.

'What happened then, as I saw it, was that suddenly Hawthorn as he drew just in front of Macklin, pulled over to his right violently to stop in his pit. Lance had to pull over to his left to avoid hitting Hawthorn's car. I think Lance expected him to go whizzing by. Instead of that he pulls in front of him, stands on everything (*brakes violently*) and Lance has to take

108

immediate and violent action to stop from hitting the Jaguar up its chuff. Levegh clouted the Austin-Healey and knocked the car spinning right up the track.

'There was an explosion. I saw the Mercedes was airborne. And then there was a second bang and the car disintegrated. Looking down, I saw bits of it going in all directions, but mainly to the left. That was towards the open public enclosure immediately before the main grandstand. Kinetic engergy sent bits of the suspension and other pieces of the motor car flying into the crowd. At the same time I heard a great scream. A sort of unison scream. And then, I recall, everything went completely silent for a few seconds. I think it was shock. And then the screams and shouts and the realisation all started again. People standing with friends, families that had been mowed down, bodies broken up like pieces of the motor car, suddenly realised what had happened. And the terrible screaming went on.

'My viewpoint on the pits more or less overlooked this enclosure. There was a lot of smoke around and there was burning, straw bales were burning. I looked down and I could see that what had been a crowd was no longer a crowd. There had been several hundred standing there, but now nobody was standing. Some were attending to others. They were all either kneeling or lying.

'I looked down, quite dumbfounded and thought, *"What are we doing it for? Why do we go motor racing when things like this happen?"* And I stood there, looking, not knowing really what to do. The race was just carrying on.

'To my right was a body. It was Levegh's body, just against the barrier on the left-hand side of the road. So when his car broke up his body had been jettisoned and had gone forward more or less as far as Lance's car went forward. It seemed to be smouldering and smoking, and some of the straw bales and advertising banners were burning right where his body was lying.'

In this Leston was mistaken according to other witnesses. They say the body was that of a woman. A flying hub cap from the Mercedes, hurtling with incredible force, had picked her up by her dress and whirled her to death on the track.

Lofty England, running the Jaguar pit, was standing on the counter, saw the Jaguar and the Austin-Healey and the Mercedes arrive and the crash. Hawthorn coasted past the pit, he says, and stopped at the Cunningham pit, three pits up. 'He got out,' says England, 'expecting, as I expected, to see about six more cars run into this lot. If you ever see an accident in front of the pits the first thing you think is, "Christ! This is only the start. There's going to be the most almighty pile-up." Hawthorn had seen Levegh fly out of his car. He had seen all those people mown down. It wouldn't make anybody very happy.'

England was then confronted with the fact Hawthorn's Jaguar was three pits up the road. The race regulations forbade him from putting the co-driver, Ivor Bueb, in at that point. The car was not allowed to be reversed or even pushed back to the Jaguar pit, the only place where a change of drivers was permitted. So, he says, 'I took Hawthorn back to the car and said, "Do one more lap and we'll put Bueb in." He did it. He was a chap who did what he was told.'

*   *   *

Artur Keser missed the actual accident. He explains: 'I was in one of the little restaurants, a tent, sipping champagne with the boys, the journalists, because I like champagne and I knew they liked it, too. We were near a television set. It was in the bar of this tent, just behind our pit, and suddenly we heard a terrible shock. Crash! This was really like a bomb. I have seen crash tests at sixty kilometres an hour and the sound is always the same. And when something is travelling at nearly three hundred kilometres, it must sound, as this did, like a cannon. On the television screen I saw black smoke. The TV was not very good, but I saw people running around, and suddenly – Neubauer in the middle of the road. He was waving his jacket with one hand and gesticulating furiously with the other.

'I said to the boys, "Listen, something has happened. Please step back I have to go and see . . ." So I went to the spot. I saw Levegh's car and the rescue workers trying to put sand on it. And later I said to Neubauer, "What the hell were you doing in the middle of the road?" I believed that he was trying to help

Faroux who also tried desperately to try to slow the race, because the battle fever was so high . . . the drivers didn't realise what had happened. How bad it was. So I asked Neubauer, "Why did you do it? It was so dangerous. I was preparing to release the story of how you were run over by a racing car at Le Mans, the glorious end of Alfred Neubauer." And he replied, "There, you see how stupid you are." (We were always fighting each other.) "You are too stupid to realise what happened. When Macklin's car came spinning round, we all ran away, and the only safety, the only place to run at that moment was in the middle of the track. Because at that moment there were no cars coming round." Then cars began to race up from the White House, and the refugees from the Macklin spin ran back across the pit road. But Neubauer couldn't move so fast. He was too fat at that time. He drank too much champagne. And in sheer self-defence he began to wave at the oncoming cars, with his jacket, and then with his hat, his famous hat, in his other hand, trying to attract the attention of the drivers.

$$* \qquad * \qquad *$$

The stricken area was like a battlefield. Horrified men and women tried desperately – dreading what they might find – to discover if friends or relatives were among the victims. Ambulance men and Army doctors, called to the scene, had to fight their way through the crowd to start the rescue work. Geoffrey Dickson and Duncan McDermott, from the Hammersmith hospital, left their grandstand seats to join in. They had ceased being spectators and were now doctors. Bodies lay everywhere on the blood-soaked ground. Fencing was torn up for stretchers.

A young man emerged from the devastation. He was carrying his girl friend. She was dead. But the young man was whispering in her ear. A woman, her arm smashed, was screaming as she held the body of her son as he lay beside her husband. The man was dead. Priests who had planned to say open-air Mass next day, hurried to comfort the injured and give the last rites to the dying.

The race went on. Tom Wisdom, heading for the pits in his Bristol at 130 mph saw the Mercedes leap into the air and the torrent of fire and fragments it spewed. He wrote in the *Daily*

Herald: 'I didn't sense the full horror then. I saw cars sliding crazily about in front of me and smoke and fire. Until I had got round them, I was in the grip of my own reactions. Then I was past, and what I had seen came back to me slowly – one grim detail after another.'

For Hawthorn, driving on his extra lap to bring his Jaguar back to the pits, for Wisdom and the other drivers passing the accident spot, there was another shocking moment to come. Between Arnage and the White House there was another wrecked car, another rising column of black, oily smoke, and another gout of flame, Dick Jacobs' MG had crashed. He had a fractured skull, a couple of broken ribs, a broken leg, and severe burns.

*   *   *

Erik Johnson and his little party, having moved away from the place where they had been unable to see, found their way to the tribunes, the public area above the pits. He recalls: 'I was standing on top of the Mercedes pit when it happened. The first two hours of the race had been an absolute ding-dong between Fangio and Hawthorn. They were going at it as if it were a five-lap sprint in a club race at Silverstone.

'There was a gasp from the crowd. I looked to the left and saw the remnants of Levegh's car rising up the bank and the engine and gearbox depart from the front of the car and fly out. They seemed to fly along the chestnut paling fence at about head height, parallel with the fencing and then went into the crowd. That was at the spot we had left. There was a lot of smoke, but the picture I saw will stay with me as long as I live. I saw Macklin spinning, and I saw him jump out. But his car was partially blocking the road in front of the pits. I remember seeing two German mechanics in the Mercedes team push a trolley jack across the circuit, pump it up, and push the car out of the way. It was the bravest thing I ever saw. There was smoke everywhere, the race was still going on, although officials were trying to get it under control, putting out yellow flags to get the cars to slow down.

'I was rooted to the spot. There was nothing one could do. One was in a crowd and it was difficult to get down. Police and race marshals had a really incredibly difficult job to try to clear a way through the carnage. I remember they found the body of a photographer from almost opposite the barrier where I was standing. The police were stopping everybody from crossing the circuit. Many people lost all interest in the outcome of the race and tried to leave. They were jamming the exits. It was eight or nine o'clock at night before we managed to get out and go back to our hotel. We found we couldn't get a phone call through to England for love or money to tell our families that we were all right. It was horrific because one looked in the French papers, like *L'Équipe* and saw that they had long lists of casualties. But for some, in place of names, they would put *type Anglais*. That was the only description they could give. We were scared that the Sunday papers at home would pick up these descriptions and frighten our families.'

Peter Jopp was standing on the counter of the Lotus pit at this, his first Le Mans. The first thing he saw of the disaster was the Mercedes go up in the air. He rushed down and went through the tunnel to the stricken spot to see if he could help, together with many other people. 'I had never seen anything like it,' he said. 'I hadn't been involved in any wartime experience with bodies lying around. The only way I can describe it is by saying it was a clear patch with lots of bits. There obviously wasn't anything I could do. It seemed somehow to be very quiet. At any rate, I didn't get the impression of screaming. Such noise as there was came from the cars racing past. And even there, on the spot, I didn't realise that more than eighty people had been killed and lord knows how many injured.' It seemed to Jopp that to stay where he was might mean that he would get in the way of those who could be doing some good. Besides, he had a job to do in his pit. He turned and walked away . . . to the race that was still going on.

*   *   *

Macklin ran some fifty yards in the direction of the wrecked Mercedes and the body on the track about 150 yards away. 'Some people,' he says, 'thought that I was running back to see if I could do anything about the person lying beneath the Mercedes. I wasn't. I thought – wrongly – that it was the driver. I thought it was Fangio or even Stirling, because I knew they were sharing a car. I didn't know that Levegh was anywhere near me. I thought it was sad, but even from that distance I could see there wasn't anything I could do. I was running to get out of the way of being involved in another accident if a car should come rushing through at high speed in a few seconds and hit the Austin-Healey. And then I saw Tommy Wisdom's Bristol coming quite slowly through the pall of smoke and the flames where the Mercedes was burning. And when I realised how slowly he was going through the pits area, and then saw him accelerate away, I thought they must have the yellow warning flags out, and he could see what's happened, so there's no chance now of anyone coming racing through.

'So then I turned and walked back the other way, to my pit in the direction of the Dunlop Bridge. And as I walked along the earthen bank I could hear the exclamations from the crowd a few feet away: *"Quelle horreur!" "C'est affreux!"* How frightful! How ghastly! I had often found myself reacting against the crowds who thronged to motor races on the Continent. Not so much in England, where they went to see motor sport for the same reason that I was taking part in it, the fun and the skill of it. Most of them on the Continent, it seemed to me were there only to see an accident. And when I heard them shouting how terrible it was, I felt like shouting back, "Well, that's why you came isn't it?" And in that moment I realised that I hated the crowd.

'When I reached the point opposite my pit the cars were coming through very slowly, and then gradually accelerating round the Dunlop Bridge corner. I jumped off the bank, and when there was nothing coming I just ran across the road and jumped on to the pit counter. Donald Healey came up and said, "Christ Almighty, Lance, what happened?" I said, "That bloody idiot, Mike Hawthorn – I don't know what the hell he was up to, but he just suddenly pulled straight across in front of me and clapped his brakes on." I didn't know just what had happened behind me. Nor, I think, did anyone else around in that part of the pits area. It was some two hundred yards from the accident. You can't really see from that distance. Donald asked if I was all right, and I told him, "I'm bloody

114

lucky to be all right, but I am." I added, "I'm afraid the car's rather badly damaged." Donald was quite nonchalant about it. "Oh, I shouldn't worry about the car," he said. "You must be a bit shaken. Let's go and have a drink to celebrate your escape." So we went off to a marquee behind the pits; and Donald's son, Geoff, came with us, and Rosa, the girl I had pretended to marry in Nassau. My brother-in-law, the Duc de Caraman, was there too. Donald ordered a bottle of champagne and we sat down and started drinking.

'The first I knew that something really serious, something of unusual proportions in a motor-racing accident, had happened, was when Les Leston suddenly appeared. He had gone across the track through the pedestrian tunnel and walked straight into the middle of the carnage. He came up to our table and burst out, "Oh my God, you've never seen anything like it! It's like a bloody butcher's shop out there. There are bodies everywhere. Bits and pieces! It's a terrible sight." I exploded at him "Les, for Christ's sake! It's people like you who give motor racing a bad name. You exaggerate so much." He stared at me and said, "I'm not joking. There must be a hundred people killed." I couldn't believe it. "For God's sake, Les," I said, "don't be ridiculous. The car didn't even go into the crowd." But he insisted that it was bad, and we all began to accept that it did sound nasty. And one or two more people began to trickle in saying how terrible the accident was. One man told of coming out of the lavatory, not even knowing there had been an accident, to be confronted with a procession of people going past carrying arms, legs and torsos.

'And then a mechanic who had worked for the HWM team for which I had driven in Formula One races, and who was now with Jaguar, came up and said, "Lance, would you come in to the Jaguar pit and have a word with Mike Hawthorn? He's having hysterics and says that it's all his fault, and he's got the deaths of all these people on his conscience. He is saying he's never going to race again." I said, "I don't honestly think I could do any good if I did come and talk to Mike Hawthorn, because he bloody nearly killed me too, and I'm not feeling all that happy towards him." The mechanic mumbled that he was sorry I felt like that, and went away.

'A few minutes later the door of the Jaguar pit opened and

115

Mike emerged. He staggered the twenty-five yards to where we were sitting. He was tottering. He stood behind me at the table, put his arm on my shoulder, and said, "Oh my God, Lance, I'm terribly sorry. I bloody nearly killed you, and I killed all those people. I'm really sorry. I'm certainly never going to race again." Donald said, "Mike, for Christ's sake pull yourself together." And, looking at Hawthorn, my anger evaporated. I told him that in a racing car travelling at 150 mph anything could happen, and I didn't hold it against him. Finally somebody from the Jaguar pit came and led him away into a caravan they were using as their headquarters behind the pits. I'm told that he was there for about two hours. When he came into the marquee he said he wasn't going to get into the car again. But when Bueb finished his run, Mike took over again. I think Lofty persuaded him.'

*   *   *

François Jardell did all he could to help the injured at the disaster spot. Then ambulances began to arrive from little side roads at the back of the grandstands. And expert help appeared. Stunned with the horror of the disaster, he made his way back to the pits. He screamed, 'What are you doing? Going on with your race? Are you mad?' Across the road from the accident, the pits were almost in another world. Only a relatively small number of people grasped what had happened. He tried to explain just what had happened, what he had seen. Jean Lucas brought his Ferrari into the pits. He stood listening to Jardell. Then he winked, not realising the situation, not understanding, not taking in the blood on Jardell's clothes, and said, 'You are not going to make a fuss about such a little corner of the street accident, are you?' Lucas' wife was there. She was one of the few who knew that what had happened was catastrophic, she had listened to Jardell. And when her husband uttered his half-joke, half-sneer, she drew her arm back and slapped his face. 'You see,' says Jardell, 'he did not realise . . .' Jardell decided that he would telephone his mother in Paris to reassure her about his safety. Then he began to search for his girl. He had not seen her at the disaster spot. But she seemed to have disappeared. His search took him to hospitals, to clinics, to places

116

where hastily improvised wards were set up. The world began to hear about the Le Mans disaster. But at the track it remained a strictly local affair. Over most of the course little or nothing was known of the accident.

Jardell could not understand why the race was still going on. The race authorities faced a desperate dilemma. Should they stop the race in view of the enormity of the tragedy which was becoming apparent? But what would happen? There would first be a rush to the spot. Then there would be a giant exodus from the circuit, hopelessly jamming the narrow roads for miles around. There were obvious acute dangers. The rescue work, getting people to hospital, would become impossible. And yet, when you know that scores have been killed and scores more seriously injured, how do you keep a motor race going? Charles Faroux said afterwards that only a Government edict could have stopped the race. This was palpable nonsense, and Faroux need not have uttered it. The race organisers were perfectly capable of stopping it. They decided that the reasons for stopping the race were not as compelling as the reasons for continuing. And so the cars continued to circle the Le Mans track.

*   *   *

If Pat Mennem of the *Daily Mirror* was looking for hard news, as distinct from a specifically motor-racing story, what he saw from the Girling equipage just below the start line, gave it to him. He got a momentary impression of the accident . . . 'Next moment I saw a conflagration. It was a ball of fire hurtling into the crowd. It just went zooming, this horrible ball of fire, into the crowd. I ran out of the Girling stand down behind the pits.

'The first thing I saw was Mike Hawthorn running around, white-faced, absolutely distracted. He was alone, running through the caravans behind the pits. Just running round. He must just have got out of his car.

'My object was to get to the other side of the track. The police and officials were trying to stop people from crossing, but – and I can't quite remember how I managed it, certainly not by the tunnel – I did get across. The panic was indescribable, everybody milling around. At the bottom end of the stands it

117

was quite horrific, everybody was in a terrible state. It was like a battlefield. It was arms and legs and people dying. There was nothing I could do. Elementary first aid, yes. But this was way beyond me.

'*The extraordinary thing was that five hundred yards up the road, no more, a crowd was gathered around a mock auction, It was going on as if nothing had happened.* . . .

'I saw a photographer taking pictures and I spoke to him in my best French, which is pretty appalling – and he replied in a strong Welsh accent. He was a photographer for a Welsh paper, but he was at Le Mans on holiday. I said. "I'd like to buy your films." So we negotiated, and I bought them. There was a building where you could telephone on the other side of the pits, so I rang the *Sunday Pictorial,* as it was then called, the *Daily Mirror*'s sister paper, which of course, goes to press on Saturdays. I said I'd bought these pictures, and they said I was to get back to Paris as quickly as I could and put them on the wire at our Paris office.

'I put over an initial story and then got to the town of Le Mans. I say I got to Le Mans. But to this day I can't remember how, in all that havoc, I did it. I think I must have cadged a lift, or hitch-hiked. I've a vague idea that I got on a bus for part of the four or five miles from the circuit to the town. One sounds terribly vague about it now, but there was such pandemonium it was unbelievable. But I got there.

'I walked to the Place de la République and I passed Gruber's, the famous restaurant, which was deserted. And there was a taxi driver in a Citroen Light Fifteen, with his beret and smoking his Gauloise. I suppose he'd always wanted someone to come up and say "Take me to Paris!" But nobody ever had. I said, "Take me to Paris!" He looked amazed. I said, "Yes, I want to go to Paris. How much is it going to cost?" He told me. I can't remember exactly what it was, about £40, something like that, there and back. A lot of money, those days, anyway. I said, "OK, off we go!" So I got into this motor car, and, of course, I wanted him to drive like mad. But the wretched man was obviously trying to preserve his Citroen Light Fifteen, which he was clearly very proud of, and he drove terribly slowly, and I was urging, "Come on, get a move on!" He never did more than 50 mph at his fastest. I was watching the time, not the speedometer, because time is vital if you are trying to get a story and pictures to a newspaper.

'I got him to stop at Chartres because I wanted to phone the office and tell them how I was getting on, and what the form was. So we stopped at a hotel there – I can't remember it's name – and there was a wedding party going on. I asked, "Can I make a telephone call?" But all everybody wanted to do was throw their arms around me and get me involved in this wedding party, thrusting drinks on me. I had the greatest difficulty in persuading them that all I wanted to do was to make a telephone call to England.

'We got to Paris at last, and put the photographs over. And then I decided that we ought to have something to eat. The only place open then was Les Halles, now vanished, the Covent Garden of Paris. I was a bit short of money, by this time, so I said to my taxi driver, "I think we'll have something fairly light to eat, don't you?" He looked at the menu, and there was everything on it. Lobster Thermidor and so on. And he went through the whole flaming lot. He had an enormous meal. And all I had was an omelette, because I reckoned it was all I could afford. We got back to Le Mans eventually and I managed to pay my driver. And then I was absolutely skint. But Peter Stephens, head of the *Mirror* Paris office, organised some money for me from one of the French correspondents. And then I started writing about what had happened.'

*   *   *

While Pat Mennem was on his way to Paris, Artur Keser was trying to find out what had happened to Pierre Levegh. He knew the French driver and his wife. 'After an hour,' said Keser, 'there was no news of him. Madame Levegh asked me, "Could you see what has happened. Is he dead or not dead?" So I went around trying to find him. I thought that he must have been killed immediately. There was fire, and I thought that Levegh might be lying somewhere unrecognised. It was right that I should be the one to search, for I had seen him immediately before he started the race. He wore blue trousers, and very light shoes, like tennis shoes, in order to run faster to the car in the Le Mans start, because he was already nearly fifty years old. So I knew what he was wearing, and I knew, especially, his crash helmet. He had ordered a special helmet, that was oversized, and it was the helmet worn by the jet-fighter pilots of the United States Air Force. And when I went with him to the start, I asked him, "What the hell sort of helmet is that?" And he answered, "This is a wonderful helmet. It is special protection."

'So I searched. First I entered an improvised sort of hospital centre, a small one. There were about twenty bodies heaped upon each other. I looked at them, and I would have recognised the shoes, but Levegh was not among them. I left this hospital tent which was on the pits side of the track, and went through the tunnel to the other side. And that led me to one of the worst moments of my life.

'There were people crouching over the dead and injured. They were not friends or relatives, you understand. They wanted to look. They wanted to see blood. The French police were hitting them with the flats of their sabres to make them give way and let the stretchers come through. It was terrible. It haunts me still. I have told the story sometimes to very good friends, but never publicly before. It was worse than anything I saw during the war.

'I went back to the other side of the track. There were some stewards around. I told them, "I am looking for Pierre Levegh. For his body." One of them told me, "Levegh has been taken to hospital. We put him in one of the first ambulances. He was unconscious." I said, "It's very odd," because I would have expected that we would have heard by now if Levegh was in hospital. At that moment I saw a man walking around with a crash helmet. It was unmistakably Levegh's. I said, "Hey, that is Levegh's crash helmet. Give it to me and I will take it to Madame Levegh." He came and showed me the helmet. I won't tell you in so many words what lay inside. I asked the man, "Will you please wash it out?" He did, and then I took it back to Madame Levegh. Levegh really was in hospital, but with half his head missing. I told her, "There is no hope." She was very brave. But I think she must have expected something like this. She certainly did not like his driving all those years.'

Win Le Mans? Never.

120

There was nothing to keep Madame Levegh at Le Mans. She went home. She was free of race tracks now.

The race went on.

*   *   *

François Jardell went to a hospital looking for his girl. She wasn't there. But he left something for which they were grateful. He has a rare blood group. And he gave his blood for the injured. He went to another hospital. From ward to ward, bed to bed. In vain. He didn't want to look at lists of the dead, not until he had exhausted every possibility of finding her alive. And then he went to the clinics around the district that were crowded with injured from the disaster. From ward to ward, bed to bed. As the evening merged into night it became possible for the authorities to issue lists of injured and where they might be found. At last he found the name he wanted. He went to the clinic where she had been taken. She was unconscious when, at 10 pm, he stood at her bedside. She had been wounded by flying debris and her skull was fractured. Her lips were moving. Jardell bent close. Very faintly she was whispering ceaselessly, *"Number three . . . Number twelve . . . number thirty . . ."* It took him a moment to realise that in her coma she was repeating the numbers of the racing cars, running through her mind like a film. But he felt an immense relief that she was alive. He went away to make a difficult phone call to her mother. She had never liked him.

*   *   *

Ivor Bueb brought the Jaguar in to the pit and Mike Hawthorn got into it and resumed the race. He wrote later: 'I said that I was not going to drive again, but Lofty said quite firmly: "Oh yes you are! You're going out there and finish the race. It's the only thing you can possibly do!" '

Bueb had just shown how good a driver he was. And now Hawthorn settled down to pick up where he had left off. Lofty England had told him that he had to drive. Very well, that was what he would do. It was still Jaguar against Mercedes. And why should a German beat a British car?

Meanwhile, with that duel going on, we will let Lance Macklin take up his story again : 'Somebody came up – I think it must have been my brother-in-law – and said that the accident had been on French television, and that I had been reported killed. He said, "The chances are that your mother was watching. You'd better let her know you're alive." It was impossible to get near a phone on the circuit, so Rosa, my brother-in-law and I drove into Le Mans in company with ambulances whose sirens kept up a continuous shriek. Even in the town it was difficult to get to a phone, and then as difficult to get through, but I managed it at last. My mother had indeed been watching the race on TV, and had heard that I had been killed. And then the phone rang in her villa in the south of France and she heard my voice. At first she thought it was a ghost!

'Then I went back to the circuit. I saw Earl Howe, who was the elder statesman of British motor racing, and he said, "Lance, I think you should see the organisers. This is a very serious accident. It would be a good idea if you made a brief statement to them about what happened before you disappear." So off I went to the organisers, the Automobile Club de l'Ouest. They said that there was now an official police inquiry, and would I please talk to the police?

'And then I met Juan Fangio. First he told me what had happened to him. "One moment," he said, "the road was completely blocked in front of me, and I thought *this is it!* There wasn't any room anywhere. There was Mike Hawthorn on one side, you spinning round in the middle of the road, and Levegh hitting you, and I thought *oh my Christ, I'm going straight into the whole lot*! All I could do was to hit the brakes and hope for the best. And as I hit the brakes, your car spun and the gap just opened out. I put my foot down on the accelerator and went straight through the gap without having to alter course at all."

'Fangio said something else too. "You know that this is a very terrible accident. But let's face it, if motor racing is going to go on, we must be careful not to make anybody responsible for the thing. It's much better to play it down and say you can't tell who is to blame for an accident that happens in motor racing – things go much too fast." I said, "I quite agree. There's no point in trying to put the blame on anybody in particular."

122

And so I went to the police and made a very cool statement that Mike pulled across me, and I pulled out to pass him and Levegh hit me. And both Fangio and I refused to write any articles or give any statements at the time, despite great pressure.

'The thing that surprised me was a couple of hours or so after the accident all the Mercedes trucks were lined up outside their pits, and they were packing up all their gear. They were putting tyres and all the pit paraphernalia into the trucks, so it was obvious that they were going to withdraw from the race.'

Macklin went back to Le Mans town with Donald Healey. They had dinner, and then Macklin went to bed. 'I don't think I slept very well,' he says, 'but even then it didn't really dawn on me just how serious it was. As far as I was concerned, the accident hadn't been all that terrible. I'd often spun on a race track before.'

*   *   *

The whole world knew of the Le Mans disaster long before the great mass of people all around the circuit. Again Artur Keser reveals the dramatic story of what was going on behind the dreadful scenes caused by the accident.

'Around 8 pm, the whole thing was being discussed on German television. And one of the commentators was bitterly ciritical of us. Mercedes, he said, had not even the delicacy, the sensitivity, to admit that they had killed people. Why don't they withdraw from the race?

'In Stuttgart the top Mercedes people were telephoning each other and discussing the accident, the terrible thing that had happened. So at about, I would say, 9.30, Dr Fritz Nallinger, the Chief Engineer, telephoned from Stuttgart telling Neubauer to stop. We were talking to Faroux about an eventual retirement when we more or less got the instruction to quit. I was there with Uhlenhaut and Neubauer. And Faroux implored us to continue. Ambulances were still going to and fro between the circuit and the hospital. If Mercedes quit, they would have to give an explanation and reveal over the whole circuit what had happened. The result could be very dangerous. When people learned that there were sixty-five dead, which was the

123

figure at that time, they would come rushing to the main stand. In fact it was not until half an hour after midnight that the first official announcement of the accident was made over the loudspeakers. I heard it. Faroux implored us to stay in. The race had to go on. I cannot blame him.

'Neubauer had received the instruction from Nallinger. But I was in higher contact. We were fighting for a continuation. I had seen all the Grands Prix the year before, and the start of the Grand Prix season in the Argentine in '55, but this was a battle such as we had never seen even in a Grand Prix before. The first two hours were a real dog fight. It was us and the Jaguars. The Italian challenge was broken. And there were all these lousy little things, the smaller, slower cars, in between. The differential in performance between the cars sharing the circuit, the Austin-Healey as well, that was where the trouble was. They were nearly half the velocity of the big cars. Even so, they were fighting, because they knew each other very well, all the boys. We wanted to carry on. We were in a kind of battle fever, because now everything was going smoothly again. The race was going on. And we knew that eventually the Jaguars would be in trouble because they would not slow down.

'I said that I would telephone Dr Nallinger to put all this to him, and Neubauer agreed. I told him that Faroux had implored us to carry on. He said, "Well, that goes against the order I gave. Now you must speak to the managing director." This was Dr Fritz Koenecke. But I couldn't get him then. He was on another line. Through Nallinger he asked me to call him back. But neither he nor I had realised how difficult that would be. The pressure on the telephone system was tremendous. People were having to tell relatives and friends that they were all right; and of course the same was true of incoming calls with a flood of inquiries. It took me an hour and a quarter, and a lot of money, to reach Dr Koenecke at about 11.30. He was in Stuttgart waiting for my call, because it was virtually impossible to get through to Le Mans.

'Finally I got Koenecke, and what he said to me I will remember all my life. He said, "I will not give you an order to withdraw from the race. I will try to convince you. One question: What will you do tomorrow, Sunday afternoon at four o'clock when the race ends? Will you stop the car one minute before the end of the race in order to make a gesture? Will you win? What will you do to show you are happy to have won? What sort of figure will you cut?" And I said, "Well, I must admit that this is a difficult question." And while I was thinking of this, he said, "Look, I understand. You are really in the thick of battle. But we are outside, here in Stuttgart. We are the general staff, and we have all discussed this together. We are not in the battle-line. The whole Board have talked to each other by telephone, and say whatever you like about how it happened, it is a Mercedes car that has killed seventy people" – which was then the known death toll. So I said, "But it was a Frenchman, Levegh . . ." He wouldn't let me say more. "It doesn't matter. It was a Mercedes car. And we think that the only gesture we can make is to retire from the race and bow in respect to the dead. You cannot be sure that you will win. But even if you do, you will make a crude and unsympathetic figure."

This was a discussion that lasted more than half an hour. Because I was fighting to stay in the race. Because I am not the man to accept an order unless I am properly convinced. I said to Dr Koenecke, "What are we left with if we retire? In the annals of Le Mans it will always say that Jaguar won the race. It will not be recorded that *Mercedes retired very bravely*." His answer was, "That kind of thinking makes no sense. We will just have to take it." Finally I said, "Well, Dr Koenecke, I must admit that you are right."

'I went back to Neubauer in the pits and said, "Stop the whole thing. We cannot continue." Uhlenhaut was there. He was always very pro-British – he is half English. He said, "Before we officially retire, we should tell the Jaguar people. We can't let it come to them as a surprise, because they might say, you could have told us, we want to retire as well."

'We went to the Jaguar pit and arrived just as they were changing drivers. Mr England was very busy. He didn't seem to hear all that was said. All he got of what Uhlenhaut was telling him was "we are retiring." So instead of wanting to know our reasons, what had decided us, and considering, perhaps, if Jaguar should eventually retire as well, he turned to his drivers and said, "They retire. You can take it easy." This is not an accusation, if that is the right word. I am not

125

criticising Mr England for this. It was understandable. Because Jaguar was possessed by the same battle-spirit as we were. We might perhaps have reacted differently . . . And the Jaguars continued the race.'

Lofty England recalls: 'They came to me at a quarter to one in the morning. They told me that their directors had been on the phone to them and that public feeling in Germany was so high that they felt that they should withdraw their motor cars, and that they intended to do it at one o'clock in the morning. And what did I intend to do in those circumstances? My reply was that we had gone on running some seven hours since the accident, and I was satisfied that the organisers were quite right to continue with the race. And as we had continued I could see no point in withdrawing, and if they were going to withdraw, I was not. I made it absolutely clear. Did I refer to London? No. It was my job. I was running the race. I ran motor racing on the basis that I was responsible for every decision. No other way to run a railway.'

Uhlenhaut and Keser had delivered their message and received Jaguar's answer. Keser goes on: 'We went back to Neubauer. He wanted to continue until 4 am, because that would be halfway through the race. One of our cars was leading, then came two Jaguars and then our remaining car. By four o'clock Neubauer believed that both our cars would be in front of the Jaguars. But Uhlenhaut and I said, no, we had promised Dr Koenecke. And then Neubauer flagged them in.'

It was 1.45. The Mercedes were lying first and third with a Jaguar in second place. How did the drivers of the German cars feel about it? Stirling Moss believes that the withdrawal was due to the insistence of John Fitch, Levegh's co-driver. Moss said: 'John Fitch felt that in deference to those who had died, Mercedes should withdraw their cars. Now if the authorities had decided to stop the race that would have been a reasonable solution. But they had decided not to, in their wisdom, and I can see why they didn't. Stopping the race wouldn't have helped anybody. It would have done no good whatsoever. But Fitch felt that because a Mercedes was the car involved, Mercedes should step out. He kept saying that we should ring Stuttgart and get the directors out of bed. He was upset. Everybody was upset. I respect his thoughts but I didn't agree with

126

them. I don't think it did any good. In fact, the withdrawal led to some of the rumours about the Mercedes cars that have persisted so long.' And Fangio? He told me: 'Our car was in the lead, so I was not opposed to leaving the race. If we had not been in the lead, I would have been against it.'

But let us return for a while to Artur Keser. He said: 'Neubauer tried to put all the blame for the accident on to Hawthorn, but this was entirely wrong. The terrible thing was that Levegh – and all those people in the crowd – should not have died. There was enough room for him to have got through. Levegh was the typical Le Mans driver, the man who just goes out for the glory of Le Mans. It was quite different to be in with the bunch who were fighting so desperately in the first two hours of the race. Levegh really had no business to be in that company, that is the point. He was in a different class. Fangio said that in that first moment, just before the accident, Levegh saved his life by throwing up his arm to indicate trouble. But later, thinking about it, we came to the conclusion that it was a gesture of sheer despair. It is probable that he saw the end.'

*   *   *

At dawn an appropriate melancholy drizzle set in at Le Mans. Before a crowd numbed into indifference, or merely snatching a fitful sleep, the Hawthorn–Bueb Jaguar was leading the race. Then came a Maserati, the Collins–Frere Aston-Martin, then the Rolt–Hamilton Jaguar, which was followed by the Claes–Swaters Jaguar. The Beauman–Dewis Jaguar, if anybody cared, had long gone into the sandbank at Arnage, where it defied its driver's efforts to dig it out. There were only twenty-five cars still racing at 8 am, and nobody was being thrilled by anything that was happening on the circuit.

The lists of the dead were virtually complete. Among the names were Jack Diamond, the young racing enthusiast from Edgware, London, and Robert Loxley, from Worcester, who had stayed at the enclosure that Erik Johnson had left. The last body to be identified was a man. It was Pierre Levegh, the only driver to have been killed. Still working in hospital, faces lined with fatigue, were the Hammersmith doctors, Dickson and McDermott.

127

Lance Macklin awoke on that Sunday morning to a shock. It was not until he opened the newspapers, read the headlines and the stories, that he realised the full magnitude of the disaster. He thought, "Oh God, what a terrible thing," but he was just more thankful that he had escaped than anything else.

He went down to the circuit. He was stunned to see the spot where Levegh's engine and front suspension had dealt such slaughter was crowded. 'The grass was soaked with blood and there was that awful smell of death you get in the air when there has been a lot of blood around. And the place was crowded. That same spot. I suppose they thought it must be a good place to be. Perhaps there would be another accident. I had driven in Italy, France, all over Europe and in South America and Mexico. Even before this Le Mans, I rather disliked the crowds who went to motor races. To me, motor racing was a sport. I was doing it because I enjoyed it. When there was an accident and somebody got killed or put themselves into hospital, I was genuinely upset. I thought what a tragedy that such a great sport has to be spoiled by somebody being killed or maimed. But I always got the impression, especially in the Latin countries like Italy, or South America, that most of the crowd went there, as they went to a bullfight, hoping to see the matador gored to death. They went to motor racing hoping to see someone killed, or at any rate, have a bad crash. The car catches fire or goes end over end, and the driver is burned alive – that makes their motor-racing day. All this didn't apply to the English crowds, because they know more about racing. They are genuinely interested and many of them would like to be racing drivers themselves. They don't go hoping to see accidents in England. But looking in astonishment at the crowds packed in where so many had died a few hours before, I couldn't feel sorry. They had come to see me die, or my friends die. And instead eighty of them had been killed. I knew it was terrible. And my mind was horrified. But I couldn't *feel* sorry.'

*　　　*　　　*

Peter Jopp and Graham Hill – who was acting as a mechanic for the Lotus car – went to the offices of L'Automobile Club de

128

l'Ouest that Sunday, and says Jopp, 'The most sickening thing of the whole story for me was that the organisers seemed to be under pressure not from drivers and people who were involved, but from people saying, for example, "My sister was killed yesterday. Where do I claim the insurance?" '

*   *   *

The rain began to pound down. The Hawthorn Jaguar held its lead. Only eighteen cars were racing when, just before 4 pm, Faroux walked to the finish line with the chequered flag. He was still a tall, unbent figure, but this made him seem somehow pathetic, for the first time. Sadly he lowered the flag for Hawthorn's win.

Teddy Culbert, an American motor-racing enthusiast, represented the firm that presented the traditional champagne to the winning crew. It was his job to hand over the champagne as they received their garlands. The custom was for the winners to uncork the bubbly, and as it gushed out to sprinkle it liberally over the crowd applauding around them. That done, the happy pair would take a prolonged swig or two from a succession of bottles. On this occasion Culbert, bottle in hand, stared in some perplexity at Mike Hawthorn. He found it hard to decide what to do. A race in which more than eighty people have been killed was, he felt, hardly the occasion for festivities, even if you happened to have won. Hawthorn had no such inhibitions. According to Culbert he snapped, 'What are you waiting for?' and snatched the bottle from Culbert's hand. Then he began to drink as if this were just another victory.

Jacques Ickx was watching. Recalling the scene twenty years later, he said, 'It was a scandal. A disgrace. Someone should have told him that one does not behave like that in such a situation. He stood there, laughing and smiling. Yes, it was a disgrace. But Hawthorn was really like a schoolboy of fourteen. When he went into the pits at the time of the disaster, Lofty England told him to get back into the car and drive. As one would tell a schoolboy what to do. And, responding like a schoolboy, he drove. And like a schoolboy he stood there grimacing and laughing and drinking champagne.'

The French paper, *L'Auto-Journal*, published a picture of Hawthorn in the Jaguar, drinking champagne, with one arm around a beaming Ivor Bueb. The sardonic caption was, *'A votre sante, Monsieur Hawthorn!'*

The French Press, much of it anyway, at once pinpointed the responsibility. Their verdict: *'Hawthorn est coupable!'* Others decided that it had been Levegh's fault. 'Too old to drive such a fast car,' they said. And it cannot be doubted that this was so. Too old and too out of touch with the ever-increasing competitiveness of the normal motor-racing circus that was exemplified by the top drivers in the first two and a half hours of the 1955 Le Mans. And perhaps never talented enough to have held his own in that company. But having said this, it does not fix the whole responsibility on poor Levegh.

Lofty England is adamant that no responsibility can be attached to Hawthorn. He said: 'I respect Macklin's opinion. But he says that Hawthorn overtook him and was going to overshoot his pit. But he quite definitely wasn't going to overshoot. If this had been so, he would have been braking to the extent that he would have locked the wheels. There weren't any braking marks down the road from Hawthorn's car. In fact he did go past our pit, but he coasted past. You can see this in the film that Jaguar's have which shows that as Hawthorn goes past the pit, he puts his stop lights on.

'In this case I'm positive in my mind about what happened, and I've spent a lot of time on this, because a lot of nasty things were said. Hawthorn was one of the finest drivers in the world. He didn't make that sort of mistake. He'd had two laps' warning to come in. We did this with everybody. So there was no question of his suddenly deciding to come in. There was a right "line" on which to come into the pits. He had to overtake Macklin who was on the right-hand side of the road. He couldn't have come down the other side. There was no pit lane at that time.

'Now this is the important factor. At this time there was a set of conditions which, I think, you would not normally get again.

'You had Hawthorn leading Fangio by something in the region of ten seconds. He had eight seconds' lead the previous lap and he was gaining all the way. Up to this point, Levegh,

130

who was fifty years old and shouldn't really have been driving the thing, was following Kling. He had followed Kling consistently for two hours, riding round behind him. On that lap Kling ran into trouble with his accelerator control, and he pulled out between Arnage and White House corner to come into the pits, which he did. So Levegh, for the first time in nearly two and a half hours, was left out on his own with Fangio up his tail about to pass him in front of the grandstands, in front of the French crowd. The hero of the French crowd for his great effort of 1952, being lapped after two-and-a-half hours' racing by his team-mate in a similar motor car! It doesn't make him look like a champion any more. He is watching behind him what Fangio is doing. He can also see Kling behind. Macklin is watching what Levegh and Fangio and Kling are doing. Watching all those fast motor cars, much faster than Macklin's, having to keep an eye on all those people, he is unable to keep as quick an eye on the chap in front. When he talks about Hawthorn . . . Hawthorn never suddenly stopped at all. It was probably simply the fact that Macklin, quite rightly, had to watch all this stuff, because if Fangio had passed Levegh there would have been very little room. Fangio didn't. Fangio could see what was going to happen. The other thing to remember is that Fangio missed all that lot, in spite of the fact that he was right behind Levegh when the accident happened. Macklin's car went across the road, hit the pit and went back again. Fangio went through, so it was quite possible to evade it all. The accident took place on the right-hand side of the road. The whole left-hand side, from the white line across, was open. Levegh didn't use it. Because he panicked. He clapped the brakes on, and I would say the car pulled to the right, and caught and ran over Macklin's car. Admittedly Macklin pulled out sharply round Hawthorn. I think he obviously braked very heavily at the last minute and turned out at the same time.

'I saw that part – it was the first part that I could see. There was a slight bend, and I was standing on the pit counter, looking down the road, waiting for Hawthorn to come in. The first thing I saw Hawthorn arriving, and then Macklin coming out behind Hawthorn, and then Levegh arriving and shunting Macklin up the back, he going off and the car going all to pieces, and Macklin's car coming across the road, thumping some people next to us, and going to the other side.

'Hawthorn was in a car much faster than Macklin's. He went past Macklin, so he had to be going faster, and so he didn't back into Macklin. Once Hawthorn had gone past him, Macklin must have known what he was doing. Hawthorn would not have been on that line if he was going straight on. There is no blame attaching to Macklin because all these other things were happening at the same time. It's one of those things in motor racing where a particular set of circumstances can arise with terrible effect, and they did. That's what it amounted to.

'Hawthorn went past our pit and stopped three pits up at the Cunningham pit and got out, expecting, as I expected, to see half a dozen more motor cars pile up. That's the first thing you think of if something like this happens in front of the pits. So he rapidly got out through the back of the Cunningham pit.

'By this time, Macklin had walked back across the road and said to Hawthorn something like. "That was your fault." Now this, you may think, was because he believed it. But I don't think so. I think that somebody who has just been shunted up the back by a car doing 150 mph, and hit the bloody fence across the road will say, "That was your fault somebody ran into the back of me." Hawthorn had seen all this happen. He had seen Levegh fly out of his car. He had seen all those people mown down. It wouldn't make anybody very happy.

'My job then, because he had overshot our pit and you are not allowed to change drivers or push the car back, was to take Hawthorn back to the car. I told him to do another lap and then Ivor Bueb would take over. He did it. He was a chap who did what he was told.'

I asked Mr England what he felt about the evidence of those who had come across Hawthorn saying in real anguish, 'Oh, my God! I've killed all those people! What am I going to do?' To which he replied: 'I don't think that's right at all.'

Mr England had a further point. 'If there is an accident in the road and five people see it, they will all give you different stories about what happened. It depends where you see it; whether you were concentrating; and so on.'

132

The truth of this is demonstrated by his assertion that Macklin spoke to Hawthorn on crossing the road and reaching the pits, and Macklin's that the first he saw of Hawthorn after the crash was when Hawthorn came into the tent where Macklin was drinking with Donald Healey, hysterically saying that he was to blame.

The film that Mr England mentions was kindly shown by Jaguar to Lance Macklin and the author. Hawthorn's car clearly has its stop lights on from the moment it appears. It hardly seems credible, in any event, that Hawthorn, having overtaken Macklin to get into his pit, would have 'coasted' because of what was happening behind him, only putting his brakes on at the last moment. It just doesn't make sense, even if Hawthorn was shocked by what was going on behind him. One would have thought it would have been natural for Hawthorn in those circumstances to have stopped at his pit – *if he could*. Hawthorn gave his version of what happened in a mere couple of pages in *Challenge Me The Race*. He wrote: 'I overtook Kling's Mercedes just before the Indianapolis turn, and Levegh's car just after the White House where the straight run up to pits begins.

'The only car now in front of me was Macklin's Austin-Healey and as I came up alongside I worked out whether there was room to pass him and then pull in to the pits. In my view there was, so I kept on and then as the pits drew nearer I put up my hand, put the brakes on and pulled in. I was nearly there, when out of the corner of my eye I saw something flying through the air. It was Levegh's Mercedes which went cartwheeling over the safety barrier, bounced once, and disintegrated with the force of an exploding bomb. Simultaneously Macklin's Austin-Healey came past spinning round backwards, then slewed across in front of me towards the pits.

'It was all over in a second or two. . . . Dazed by what I had seen, I had let my Jaguar roll on past our pit and as reversing is forbidden I stopped it and ran back to see if Lofty England agreed to my doing another lap before coming in. He sent me off. . . . Driving mechanically, I only wanted to get out of the car and get away from the track.

'Back at the pits the track was littered with debris . . . I suppose I was near to hysteria as a result of the shock, coming on

133

top of the concentrated nerve strain of the previous two hours ...'

Hawthorn's assertion that he *'ran back to see if Lofty England agreed to my doing another lap'* is at marked variance with the recollections of others – including Mr England.

When the book appeared and extracts were published in the *Daily Express*, Macklin wrote to the newspaper: 'Mr Hawthorn says that there was ample time for him to get ahead of me before braking for the pits, that as the pits drew nearer, he put up his hand and drew in, that when a faster car passes you it is almost automatic for a driver to glance in his mirror to see if there is another one coming, but that I, taken by surprise, for some reason, pulled over to the left from which moment Levegh's plight was desperate.

'I have no desire to attack Mike Hawthorn but in self-defence I must ask you to let me state that I saw no sign being given and that in my opinion there was far from ample time for Mike Hawthorn to draw across in front of me before braking for the pit.

'By reason of this action I was compelled to pull out as I did if I was not to crash into the back of his car.

'I was, of course, aware that other cars were about to pass me as I had looked into my driving mirror *about one minute before Mike Hawthorn overtook me*.' (My italics.)

And Macklin then put in train an action against Hawthorn, alleging libel.

Fangio wrote: 'Petrified with horror, I saw the Mercedes take off as though the Austin-Healey's tail had been a springboard . . . I found myself confronted by Hawthorn's Jaguar, the first to brake and still slowing down. *The English driver had evidently not calculated his pit's position correctly, and finally stopped some eighty yards beyond it.*'* (My italics.)

Paul Frere, who shared with Peter Collins the Aston Martin that finished second in the race, and is now a distinguished motoring journalist, has written recently: 'Hawthorn was engaged in a merciless battle with Fangio and was leading the race. It would have been unthinkable that, coming out of the White House bend, about one kilometre before the pit area,

* *My Twenty Years of Racing*, Temple Press, 1961.

he should have been content with following Lance Macklin's much slower Austin-Healey. And why should he? His Jaguar was quicker round the bend and came up so fast that overtaking was a mere formality. So he overtook the slower car and moved back to the right with room to spare. Back on the right-hand side of the track he started to brake (probably about a quarter of a mile before the pit area) in order to stop at his pit.

'Macklin, however, did not see that Hawthorn was slowing down and he had a very good reason for not seeing it. For him the faster Jaguar had become unimportant; it would soon disappear out of sight. Much more important were the two Mercedes looming up behind. . . . Had he had his eyes on what happened in front of him, it would most probably have been quite easy for him to move gently left and overtake the slowing Jaguar. . . .'

Mr Frere develops essentially the argument of Mr England about Macklin concentrating on what was happening behind him rather than in front. But Macklin has a slight advantage over Mr Frere in this matter. He was immediately involved in those cataclysmic moments. Mr Frere says that Hawthorn 'had room to spare' to carry out his manoeuvre. Macklin, the man in the middle in this fraught situation, says there was not. Mr Frere's assertion that 'it would have been unthinkable' that Hawthorn should have been content to follow the much slower Austin-Healey, 'and why should he?' is astonishing. The answer is, surely, that this was not a Grand Prix. Only two and a half hours had gone of a *24-hour race*. At most it could have been a matter of a fraction under two seconds involved. Nobody has won Le Mans with a margin as small as that. However, Mr Frere, it seems to me, has given his own case away when he writes that if Macklin had been concentrating on what was happening in front of him, rather than behind, it would most probably have been quite possible for him to move gently left and overtake the slowing Jaguar. Leaving aside Macklin's insistence that he *was* doing precisely what Mr Frere says he should have been doing, having looked in his rear-view mirror a minute previously, if he was going to overtake 'the slowing Jaguar' before it reached its pit, what on earth was the point of Hawthorn's manoeuvre at all?

135

Jacques Ickx, who saw it all, says: 'It was not a Grand Prix, but the leaders were driving as though it was. Hawthorn was, quite rightly, filled with aggression, the aggression of a man who wants to win. And when he saw Macklin's Austin-Healey in front of him, despite the fact that he was going into the pits, *he simply had to pass one more car*.'

The Le Mans disaster released a shock wave throughout Europe. France at once suspended all motor sport while the authorities assessed safety measures. The Italians stopped motor racing for a time, and the Swiss and Spanish called off their Grands Prix. There was, however no interruption of motor racing in Britain and Holland.

Lance Macklin was due to drive Stirling Moss's Maserati in the Dutch Grand Prix at Zandvoort soon after Le Mans. But he felt that he could not drive because there was another place where he should be. He had known Pierre Levegh casually for years. An odd sort of man, Macklin had thought. Morose. A little sad, perhaps. Somehow the sort of man it would not surprise you to learn had been the victim of disaster. And as a driver? 'I often raced against him,' says Macklin, 'but I never took him into consideration as a contender.' Nonetheless, Macklin felt, he should not drive at Zandvoort because he should be at Levegh's funeral. Moss agreed that someone else should drive his car and Macklin went to the service in Paris. It was a lavish, even theatrical, occasion at the behest of Mercedes. Macklin says: 'I sneaked in quietly and sat down somewhere at the back. But someone spotted me – I don't know who it was – and insisted that I went to the front of the church, and there I was, with all the notables, with eyes focussed on me. I wasn't very happy about that.'

Hawthorn was not at the funeral. He was driving at Zandvoort. A section of the crowd booed him.

*   *   *

The Mercedes team departed from Le Mans swiftly and without fuss. The very speed and precision of the withdrawal seemed to lend conviction to what had been, even before the disaster, a mere rumour, hardening into a feeling among some people about the German cars. This became a firm

136

belief, especially among some of the French, which persists to this day.

This belief, never substantiated, was that the Mercedes cars, the first fuel-injection machines to race at Le Mans, used an illegal additive such as nitro-methane, to boost performance. And since the petrol used by all the cars was strictly controlled and monitored by the authorities, the illicit fuel had to be supplied from a secret reservoir in the cars.

Lance Macklin explains how this rumour began to take hold: 'Even before the race, some mathematically minded people claimed to have worked out that the Mercedes engine would not do all that well on the normal Le Mans fuel. It was their Grand Prix engine and it ran on nitro-methane, permissible in Grands Prix in those days. The Le Mans petrol was supposed to be 100 octane, but was never anything like that. It was usually 82 or 90, no higher. With that petrol they wouldn't be very fast. And then, to everyone's astonishment, when they arrived at Le Mans in practice, they were going like rockets. People said, "We don't know how they've done it. How did they get that engine to perform so well on low octane fuel?" The nitro-methane, according to the rumours, could have been secreted in the tubular chassis. I am not saying that this was so, I am merely quoting the rumours at the time and since. But I could not believe that any of the drivers knew about it, if it was so. And then, of course, the Mercedes team left the circuit very quickly, and at around five o'clock in the morning the police suddenly decided that they would like to have a look at one of the Mercedes cars. A policeman went down to the garage to impound one of the cars. But they'd gone. They rang the frontier and said that there would be a convoy of Mercedes trucks going through. They were not to let them cross. The frontier officials told the police they were too late. The convoy had gone through a quarter of an hour before.'

François Jardell says: 'I cannot, of course, be positive, but a lot of things gave me the opinion that the cars might have a little reservoir of a volatile additive. When the cars came for scrutineering' (an examination by officials to make sure that the cars conformed in the most minute way to regulations) 'I was there, and a lot of people were looking at them. But they

137

were fuel injection, new at Le Mans, and nobody could tell what they had on the cars. The scrutineers would not be looking for this. They didn't know anything about the injection system.

'I heard the first explosion when Levegh's car struck, then came a second explosion perhaps five seconds afterwards. It was really like a mine exploding. And as I have told you, there was a man in front of me killed exactly like a man killed in the war by a mine. You know, Levegh's tank was more or less empty, because it was supposed to refuel. But the fact of having two explosions, and I told it to a lot of people then, gave the feeling that the Mercedes have something different from the other cars. I was with the French armour in the war, and I saw a lot of cars blown up by mines.

'Jean Behra had told me something extraordinary. He said, "It's funny, but the Mercedes cars have a different smell, not like petrol at all." ' (Behra was to have driven a Maserati in the race, but while standing at the pit counter was injured in an incident during practice.) Jardell continued: 'One of the Mercedes drivers told us that when you wanted a boost there was a little box on the left of the car with a button which you were supposed to press, when they were for example, taking a curve.

'Ten minutes after the accident all the Mercedes mechanics were there picking up every piece of the car they could find in among the dying and the dead.

'I have nothing against Mercedes. And I cannot be sure about the fuel, but all these things impressed me, and inclined me to believe there was something wrong with the cars.

'I went back several times after the accident to see my girl friend. And I went to the police offering to testify about what had happened. I met the Prefect once and told him, "Sir, I want to testify about the fact that the explosion was just like the detonation of a mine." He said that I would be called to give evidence. But I have never been asked . . . I have never been asked . . .'

I asked Fangio what he felt about this allegation that the cars had a nitro-methane or other boost. He threw back his head and laughed. 'That's nonsense. The cars were too good to need anything like that.'

138

Mercedes, of course deny that their cars used any such additive. In the firm's Stuttgart headquarters Artur Keser told me: 'The explosion effect is explained when you consider that Levegh and the other cars were travelling at about 300 kilometres an hour, and when you come from that speed to a virtually instant standstill . . . the force of inertia was so strong that it tore the engine from the body and hurled it into the crowd. I believe that the force created would account for the blast effect. I must tell you one more thing. When I was looking at the rows of dead in my search for Levegh many at first sight appeared to have been uninjured. But when you looked more closely – and this is perhaps the answer to the man who talks of mine blasts – their heads were just a tiny bit shorter. They had all been touched on the scalp by the flying engine. It touched them and they fell. There were seventeen of them.' And that rapid, silent Mercedes withdrawal? Keser was frank. 'We were very anxious that the secrets of our fuel-injection system should not be revealed. We had the only one at that time. We didn't want to let, for example, Jaguar know all the technical details.' And Neubauer said, 'Those lousy guys, the French scrutineers, the French officials – you never know what kind of industry is behind them. When they examine our fuel injection they will learn the whole secret.'

I put the nitro-methane allegation to Stirling Moss. It was not the first time that he had heard it. He reacted with more than the typical Moss vehemence. He said: 'I am staggered at this enormous stupidity. It is not only fantastic, it is an absolute lie. The people who believe it may have been confused by the lever we used to operate the air-flap brake. A lever not a push button.

'If you take the tubes of a Mercedes 300SLR and you are able to fill them up and keep the stuff in them; if you are able to weld it so that there are no leaks; and don't forget that nitro-methane will burn through paint; if you filled the whole tubing up, I suppose it would hold two or three pints, because you are talking of tubes half an inch in diameter. It might be half a gallon. You might even get a gallon in them, though I doubt it. Now consider nitro-methane. I've raced on it. You mix it with alcohol and you put in additives, other mixing agents, acetone and castor-based oil. You mix it up to 15 per

139

cent. That gives you, obviously, a direct proportion of increase of power.

'Now if you are talking of a race twenty-four hours in length you have to realise that we were averaging 100 mph plus. We were doing something under ten miles a gallon. Therefore we were using ten gallons an hour, so that's 240 gallons, at least 240 gallons for the race. So, if the tubes held as much as a gallon, the proportion of nitro-methane would have been one two hundred and fortieth, virtually nil. Remember that you couldn't refill the tubes because you were having to refuel from the tanks at the pits under strict supervision. Then there are other little things like the metering of fuel . . . It appals me that anybody could be so' (Mr Moss's next words cannot be printed here) 'as to believe that a company like Daimler-Benz could do anything so disgraceful as cheating like that.'

Mr Moss had more to say. 'Explosions,' he said, 'let's look at that question. If you take a car doing 150 mph and a portion of that car is stopped dead in nil distance, and you have an engine weighing three or four hundredweight, then the engine is going to part company. This means that you get the snapping of high tensile matter. That is going to be like an explosion. You can get a balloon made of rubber to explode. It is ridiculous to think that a car can disintegrate, which is what happened, without there being explosions. It would have been incredible if there had not been. I would put everything that means anything to me on the line against Mercedes having cheated.'

*   *   *

The drivers and everyone else involved gave their evidence to the inquiry. 'The whole Court of Inquiry went out to the track with me,' Macklin recalls. 'We walked up and down and discussed where Hawthorn overtook me and where I put my brakes on, and where Levegh hit me, and the rest of it, quite coolly and coldly.' In Stuttgart Mercedes called an international Press conference and staged a demonstration showing that the magnesium of which so much of their Le Mans cars were constructed did not catch fire as readily as all that.

140

Jaguar issued a statement from Coventry saying that Hawthorn had been in no way to blame for the tragedy. Mercedes gave £100,000 (a tidy sum in those days) for the families of victims. Hawthorn and Macklin met from time to time, but never discussed what had happened. 'I did not want to bring the subject up,' says Macklin. 'He had come up to me and said it was his fault, and I accepted it, and that was that. I wasn't going to rub it in any way, or say "Why did you do it?" or anything like that. I refrained from pointing out to him, as I was tempted to do, that the ironic thing about the whole situation was that I actually went past the Jaguar pit in front of him. *If he had pulled in behind me he would still have got to his pit just as quickly.* I just left it at that. The only thing that did annoy me was when his book came out and he didn't say it was my fault, and he didn't say it was Levegh's fault. All he said was that it wasn't his fault. And if it wasn't his fault, it must have been somebody else's fault. That is what he more or less gave the inquiry to understand. But really the inquiry was a farce, with all of us being very muted.'

Macklin had a major worry while waiting for the inquiry findings. 'I might have found myself with enormous insurance claims to meet. More especially as the race was run on public roads. I was not only the driver – I was also the entrant of the Austin-Healey, and I believe the entrant would be responsible. It might have meant that Mercedes, Jaguar and I would have been called on to pay enormous sums. And I certainly was not insured against that sort of risk.'

*   *   *

Les Leston stayed at the circuit until the Mercedes team withdrew from the race. 'I was so upset,' he recalls, 'I didn't wait until the end. I didn't wait to see the Jaguar's hollow victory, the tragic win. I packed my bag and went back to England, still wondering why we did it – even more so when one learned that eighty or so people had been killed and Christ knows how many more maimed. I couldn't help saying to myself over and over again. "What are we doing it for? What are we trying to prove? It's an immoral, inhuman sport or business or whatever it pleases you to call it. Why are we doing it?" ' Did he ever find the answer? 'I suppose so. The answer is, because we enjoy it. When people used to ask Graham Hill why he didn't retire (years before he did) he always had the same reply. "Because I enjoy it." And – maybe it's selfishness – you keep on doing it simply because you enjoy it. Fortunately, I think, we tend to forget the terrible things, the same as we forget wars, as we forget Belsen, earthquakes. When I came back to Le Mans two years later, I didn't feel any emotion about what had happened in 1955.'

They went back to racing – Hawthorn and Macklin and the others, except Levegh, fixed eternally in position. The natural loser.

The inquiry findings came in November, five months after the disaster. Nobody was to blame, it held. No mistake was made by any competitor.

Blame? It is certain that Hawthorn set in train the events that led to the tragedy. But that is not to apportion blame. A whole series of conditions was responsible. The narrowness of the track at that point; the speed differential between the high and low capacity cars; the interweaving of countless strands of fate; and certainly of human fallibility.

*   *   *

In fact it was only by the narrowest of margins, a mere six inches or so, that the tragedy of Le Mans did not become a holocaust. When the inquiry had finished its sessions, and Macklin was waiting to drive back to Paris, he was talking to one of the technical experts who had been helping to run the investigation. He told Macklin: 'Everybody's talking about the disaster, but looking at the thing dispassionately, in my opinion it was a miracle that it wasn't many times worse.' Macklin was taken aback. It did not seem to him that what had happened could reasonably be described as a miracle. The man explained: 'Levegh's Mercedes happened to hit just six inches below the top of the tunnel cutting. That stopped the car. Six inches higher, and the whole car would have hurtled into the crowd. At the speed at which it was travelling, and with its weight and kinetic energy, and the density of the crowd, I have worked it out that there would have been at least a thou-

142

sand dead. What is more, if Fangio had hit you or Hawthorn and had gone into the pits area back somersaulting, as Levegh did, think about those two-inch thick hosepipes at every pit all with petrol under pressure. It is virtually certain that one or two of those pipes must have been torn away. Petrol would have gushed out, and there was no way of stopping it, except by climbing up to the tank high above the pits, from which the petrol was drawn. Imagine the conflagration if that had happened!'

A miracle? Be that as it may, the passage of Hawthorn, Levegh, Macklin and the others along the circuit of Le Mans had left eighty-one people dead. But two of the principal actors still had dramatic roles to play.

Why should a Kraut car beat a British car?

Mike Hawthorn did not win a single World Championship point in the 1955 season. It must have been a relief to him when it was over.

There were more traumatic moments for him in 1956. At the Goodwood Easter meeting a record crowd of more than 60,000 saw tragedy in the very first minute. A 46-year-old driver by the name of Bert Rodgers was killed when his car overturned at Lavant corner. In the third race of the day an up-and-coming 26-year-old, Tony Dennis, was driving a Jaguar borrowed from Duncan Hamilton in his first big race. The car overturned and burst into flames coming into the home straight. Dennis was thrown out and killed. In the main event Hawthorn, driving a BRM, was in second place, chasing Stirling Moss. Near Fordwater, at more than 100 mph, the BRM began to slide. It spun and hit the banking. Hawthorn knew the car was going to overturn. With the car in the air he felt himself being thrown out. And then his ankle jammed between seat and body. Somehow he broke free with the car still in the air. He landed with a shattering thud and when he had recovered his breath, he saw his car with its wheels in the air – three of them, one had been torn off. His injuries: a jarred ankle.

On the one hand the fiercest possible competitiveness, tension, life hingeing on the most precise judgments that must be made in tiny fragments of a second, close encounters with death. On the other hand . . . Here is Hawthorn's account of what happened after the Swedish Sports Car Grand Prix near Kristiansand:

144

'It would be idle to pretend that racing drivers are always the perfect guests from the hotelier's point of view, and that night the hotel's magnificent fire precautions, consisting of highly polished devices like stirrup pumps in gleaming copper-bound tubs, proved an irresistible temptation. A hosepipe battle developed in which a good deal of water fell wide of the primary objectives. . . .'

The season ended prematurely for Hawthorn on a sodden, sullen day at Oulton Park. He was driving a Lotus in a sports-car race. It slid on mud, hit the bank, and flipped. Hawthorn's injuries: a sprained ankle, ditto wrist, bruised ribs and a damaged back.

For Hawthorn 1956 was a year of escapes.

Next season he was back with Ferrari. On the plane to Buenos Aires for the Argentine Grand Prix a group of famous drivers sat down to play poker – with stakes up to £10 – Hawthorn, de Portago, Musso and Perdisa. Hawthorn lost £50 and decided that enough was enough, and indeed too much. He quit the game and Jo Bonnier took his place. By the time they had landed in Buenos Aires Musso and Bonnier had lost at least as much as they could win from racing in the Argentine.

It turned out to be a better year, if not one of his most spectacular, for Hawthorn with fourth place in the World Championship.

But 1958 was Hawthorn's year. It developed into a battle between him and Stirling Moss for the world title. There was a highly charged situation in the Oporto Grand Prix. Moss won in a Vanwall. Hawthorn was second in his Ferrari. This meant that Stirling was only five points behind Hawthorn in the championship table. In the final lap Hawthorn, trying to catch Moss, went off the road. Someone lodged a protest that in re-starting his car he had gone for a few yards against the direction of the other cars which were travelling at around 170 mph. If the protest had been upheld Hawthorn would have been disqualified and lost the points for his second place. That would have given Moss a two-points lead in the championship. But with great sportsmanship, Moss went to the stewards and told them that when he had seen Hawthorn pushing his car it had been off the track. In that case, there had been no breach of regulations. The stewards accepted Moss's evidence and the protest was rejected. Those points of Hawthorn's were to be vital to both men in deciding the championship.

It was settled in the last race of the season, the Morocco Grand Prix at Casablanca. Moss had both to win the race and put in the fastest lap, under the rules then obtaining, to have a chance of taking the title. Even then, he would not gain the championship if Hawthorn took second place. Moss went into the lead straight away with the American Phil Hill chasing him in a Ferrari. The Ferrari strategy was for Hill to press Moss, perhaps into error, and also try to achieve the fastest lap. Moss kept ahead and on the seventh lap set up a record of 2 min. 24 sec., 117·9 mph. Hill broke this record a few laps later with 2 min. 23·3 sec. Moss broke that record with 2 min. 22·9 sec. on the twentieth lap, and ten laps later he did even better with 2 min. 22·5 sec. This was the true dramatic stuff of motor racing at its best. Hawthorn was in third place with Hill second, but a long way behind Moss when on lap 36 Hill got the signal from the Ferrari pit to slow down. Hawthorn went into second place a couple of laps later. And that was how it ended. Moss had done all that could have been asked of him but was beaten – by one point.

Mike Hawthorn beat Stirling Moss by 42 points to 41. He was the first Briton to be World Champion.

Two months later Hawthorn made a shattering announcement. He was retiring from motor racing. He was 29.

He said: 'My ambition was to become World Champion. I have achieved that and I am happy.' And at a dinner of the Royal Automobile Club he said: 'I am very glad I have been able to give up motor racing although I have enjoyed it. It is not so much a question of giving up the actual driving, but of giving up the life of motor-racing drivers.'

Friends said that the real reason was that he planned to marry Jean Howarth, a glamorous fashion model. And he had long maintained that a married man should not race. It was true that he and Miss Howarth were to be married, although they did not announce this publicly. But there was another reason for his abdication. He admitted: 'The deaths of some of my colleagues and rivals recently has upset me a great deal.' In particular, the death of the brilliant Peter Collins at the

Nurburgring. Hawthorn had crowded more into a short and dazzling career than most men do in a lifetime. He had had his encounters with death. He had made his mistakes and scored his triumphs. His father had told him long ago, 'Put your heart into racing. Get to the top – then get out.' Mike Hawthorn took that advice as he had always taken his father's advice. He said: 'I have given up – but I am alive.'

*　　　*　　　*

Less than two months later Mike Hawthorn was dead.

On the wet, gusty morning of January 22, 1959, he left his garage in Farnham for London. He was going to clinch a business deal, he was lunching with friends, including holiday-camp millionaire Billy Butlin. He was driving his 3·4 Jaguar. It was a 'special' built for him by his friend, the Jaguar chief, Sir William Lyons. It had a D-type racing engine. It had a special back axle ratio. It could do an easy 130 mph. And it was finished in British racing green. He had once invited Tommy Wisdom: 'Uncle Tommy, try my car and tell me if it isn't the fastest in the world.' This morning Mike Hawthorn had plenty of time.

He came over the Hog's Back, a fastish stretch of road going over a hill leading to Guildford. An acquaintance of Hawthorn's saw the Jaguar coming towards him and was mildly surprised at its speed, close on 100 mph, he reckoned.

Another man, a friend of Hawthorn, Rob Walker, former racing driver, who ran his own racing teams and was a garage owner, had also come over the Hog's Back, having driven from his home at Frome, Somerset in his newly bought Mercedes 300SL convertible, a 140 mph car. Mr Walker stopped at the junction of the Guildford bypass, the A3. A moment earlier he had looked in his mirror and seen the Jaguar. He turned into the bypass. 'As I changed from first gear to second,' said Mr Walker, 'the Jaguar came up alongside me. The driver seemed to equal his speed with mine, turned and waved, and gave a charming smile. I recognised it was Mike Hawthorn. I turned and waved back.'

The Jaguar went past the Mercedes. 'He was going a lot faster than I was. It was pure coincidence we were there

147

together. Any suggestion that we were racing is ridiculous. Mike went on ahead of me. About 200 yards further on, past Coombs' Garage, he appeared to lose his tail. I thought he would just flick the wheel and straighten up. I'll never know what caused that skid. It was such a simple one at first. I've seen him straighten out a thousand more difficult skids on oil patches on race tracks. Eventually it was a complete side skid that went on and on. I slowed up. Next thing he had lost control. He spun round, facing me, streaking backwards. Mike disappeared across the road, clipping the rear wing of a lorry and the bumper came off, and something else flew into the air. I couldn't believe my eyes. The car hit a Keep Left traffic island, then it slewed across the verge and hit a tree. I stopped within a few seconds immediately opposite his car and ran across to it. The car was in a terrible state. For a few seconds I couldn't even find Mike. Then I saw him on the back seat with his legs out by the driver's side and his head on the passenger's side. He was still alive, but unconscious. He died before a doctor could reach him.'

How fast was Hawthorn going? Mr Walker told reporters – and the inquest – that he didn't try to estimate speeds. 'It certainly was not near 100 mph. It would have been impossible for him to reach that speed over so short a distance.'

It was a difficult thing for Mr Walker to see and believe. 'I thought Mike was immortal. Even when I saw the car crash and pieces fly in all directions, I expected him to clamber out, rub a few bruises and say, "That was another close shave." '

The tree was only nine inches in diameter. The crash uprooted it.

Standing in the forecourt of Coombs' Garage was gardener Arthur Hill. He saw two cars flashing past. A lot of spray was thrown up. He told the coroner that he estimated their speed at about 80 mph.

Lorry driver Frederick Rice said that he was going in the direction of Portsmouth. Nearing Coombs' Garage he was doing 15 to 20 mph. He had 'a faint glimpse' of a saloon car. He could not estimate its speed. 'When he was about twenty yards from me it was coming straight for me and all I could think of was to try to increase my speed to try to avoid him.' He did not feel the impact.

Rob Walker said he thought Hawthorn slackened speed when he waved. 'His speed was faster than mine,' he added. 'It was increasing at the time, and as he passed me I slackened my speed. There was a great deal of spray around and I did not want to be too close to the car, and I lifted my foot just as he passed me. Hawthorn was thirty to fifty yards ahead when the Jaguar began to break away. 'I was very surprised because I could not see any reason for it.' There was, he said, a very strong wind. 'I had just come over the Hog's Back and experienced a wind I had never experienced before in my life. It moved my car at least two yards sideways. It was almost like having a gun fired at me.'

The verdict was accidental death.

'It was ridiculous to suggest that we were racing,' said Rob Walker. No one will question Mr Walker's word. But let us go back to the Le Mans of 1955. To Hawthorn saying: 'I was momentarily mesmerised by the legend of Mercedes superiority . . . Then I came to my senses and thought: Damn it, why should a German car beat a British car?'

Hawthorn said as much to his friends with only a slight variation: 'Why should a Kraut car beat a British car?' Walker was driving a Mercedes. Hawthorn was driving a Jaguar. *Why should a kraut car beat a British car*? Mr Walker did not have to be racing for Hawthorn to ask himself that question.

Even those who had never seen a racing car were stunned. For the World Champion, a man who had survived death so many times on the track, to have died on the open road in what seemed an inexplicable accident for someone of his calibre was surely the most savage stroke of an ironical fate. Ironically, too, the Press, which had so gleefully joined in the attacks on Hawthorn at the time of the National Service uproar, now poured out the most glowing tributes. In the British way he was beatified, if not actually canonised, by death.

Stirling Moss wrote a heartfelt tribute: 'I shall try to remember Mike Hawthorn in his natural element – flat out at the wheel of a Grand Prix car. We raced together so many times that it's difficult to pick out one race as the most memorable. But one of the gayest events of the year was always the Monaco Grand Prix, and there last year, I recall, under a baking

149

hot sun and a clear blue sky, we had a tremendous duel round the houses until his Ferrari packed up. I shall always remember his tall, blond figure, clad in the inevitable green and white, stiffen to attention as he was walking disconsolately back to his pits. With great mock solemnity he jumped to a derisive but smart military salute as I went by in my Vanwall ... He raced purely for fun, and had no manager to handle his interests and problems. But everyone noticed how he was settling down. The rather trying days of his extreme youth, when he was a little given to squirting soda siphons in pubs, seemed to be over. He had become an elder statesman in the sport he loved above anything else.'

An elder statesman. One wonders what Hawthorn would have made of that?

But we must let Lofty England have the last word: 'As a person I liked him immensely. He was a chap who never let me down. He did everything you asked him to do. He wasn't searching for publicity for himself. He wasn't searching for money. He loved motor racing. We ran three motor cars for Jaguar. If anybody else ever said, "My car's not going properly," or something like that, I would say, "Take Mike's car and let him have yours." Mike and the other bloke would exchange cars, and Hawthorn would go faster than the other bloke quite naturally. He was a great, wonderful character. I liked him immensely. A man's man. The right type of bloke. The sort of man we don't see much of nowadays in this country, I regret to say.

'In 1956, the year after the disaster, we went to Le Mans again and we were the only people who ran cars with engines of over three litres. We should have been first, second and third. It so happened that we lost two cars in accidents on the second lap. Then we had trouble with the fuel injection on the remaining car, Hawthorn's. A pipe split which was very difficult to trace. By the time we sorted it out we were twenty-six laps behind. You could well say, "Why bother?" I did a quick calculation. "England, I reckon if you have a real bloody go, you can finish eighth." So I said "Mike, I'm going to have a real bloody go; I reckon we can finish eighth." He said, "Right We're on!" Now "Right. We're on!" meant that Hawthorn and Bueb would win fifteen quid each for driving another twenty

150

hours. In the bloody wet, most of it, it turned out to be. That's the sort of chap he was. There was no argument about it. "Right. We're on!" And he finished sixth. That was Hawthorn.'

Levegh . . . Hawthorn . . . Only one of the three actors is left. Let us look again at Lance Macklin.

The Survivor

Lance Macklin was soon back in action after the Le Mans disaster. It didn't affect him any more than – after the first traumatic shock – it had affected Hawthorn. What had happened to him at Le Mans was that he had had to avoid hitting Hawthorn, and in doing so had been hit in the rear and had been sent spinning down the track, narrowly escaping death. That was the limit, so far as he was concerned, of his personal involvement. The disaster had happened *behind him.*

A week or two after Le Mans he drove at Oulton Park. And a few weeks later he drove Stirling Moss's Maserati in the British Grand Prix at Aintree. And there he had a moment that brought Le Mans vividly back to him. 'There was a lot of oil and I went off the road in front of the grandstand while I was going backwards across the grass I thought, "Oh, my God, here we go again! I'm going into the bloody crowd!" But I ended up on top of some straw bales. There was straw coming down all round me. I was almost laughing with sheer relief. I felt like clucking like an old hen. I left the car because it was obviously not movable. In a major race you are not allowed to get outside assistance. If you go off the road and you get back under your own steam, that's fine. But there was no hope of my getting the car off. All four wheels were off the ground. I walked back to the pits, and I hadn't been there five minutes when Tony Rolt came in and said, "They've taken your car off the straw bales and it's just sitting there. Why don't you go back and get in it?" So I put my helmet on and ran back – it was only about 100 yards away. I got into the car and got somebody to give me a push, started it up and rejoined the race. I finished

152

eighth. They should have disqualified me, I suppose, but for some unknown reason, they didn't.'

Then came the most terrible experience of Lance Macklin's motoring career. For *him* it was far worse than Le Mans. It happened a few weeks after the British Grand Prix in the Tourist Trophy race at Dundrod. He was driving an Austin-Healey again. Macklin tells what happened:

'I was following Ken Wharton who was driving a Frazer Nash. We came up behind a German driver in a Mercedes. He was taking up an awful lot of road and we couldn't get past him. When he got to a straight section, he would pull over a bit. We couldn't pass him then because he was faster than we were, and he just pulled away from us. Then as soon as we got to some curves he was slowing us right down.

'This went on for two or three laps soon after the start of the race. I tried to get past him, but I couldn't make it, and Ken tried, but he couldn't. The next thing that happened was that a bunch of four or five Lotuses and Coopers and suchlike arrived, having caught us because we were being held up by this chap in front. He was just an inexperienced driver. He didn't know what he was doing. This bunch of Lotuses and Coopers descended on us. One of them came past me on the grass on one side, and the next moment somebody else went past on the grass on the other side. I thought, Well, this doesn't look very good, because the Dundrod circuit is very narrow, with high banks. So I thought I would just drop back a little and see what happened, because it looked a nasty situation. I dropped back some fifty yards so that I would have some sort of chance to take avoiding action if some of those chaps put a foot wrong.

'I came towards a spot called Deer's Leap, which consisted of a flat-out downhill section followed by a slight rise over the top of which you more or less took off, then went down the other side. I had the Austin-Healey flat out during this bit, doing about 140 mph, and as I came over the top of the hill, I suddenly saw a great flash in front of me. Next moment I saw cars going end over end over end and bodies being thrown into the air and cars somersaulting, and then the most enormous conflagration. There were flames everywhere. I've never seen anything like it. There were flames thirty or forty feet up

153

in the air. And I thought, "Jesus! This is it!" I didn't see how I could get out of it. There were banks on either side. There was nowhere I could go. I was going far too fast to stop, but I did manage to turn the car round through 180 degrees, braking very hard, and I went backwards into all that lot. I went straight into that great ball of fire. The whole car was surrounded by fire and I ducked right down inside. I could feel the heat and I heard a bang as the crash went on.

'Finally the car stopped and through the smoke I saw the bank quite near. I thought, "Christ! I'd better get out of here," and so I leaped out – I imagine that I'd have outleaped any deer – and scrambled on to the bank. I ran straight through the flames, but somehow although my overalls were scorched – we didn't have flameproofs then – I wasn't burned. I got on top of the bank and ran down the back. I thought my car was going to go up in flames. There were three or four other cars all round it, blazing away. There was petrol all over the road on fire, and bodies lying in the road, burning. . . .'

For Peter Jopp, too, this was far worse than Le Mans. He says: 'I was involved with Lance in the six-car pile-up at Deer's Leap. This was where Jim Mayers, a brilliant driver, was killed. His Cooper-Climax was in the middle of the road, on fire. A very up-and coming young driver, Bill Smith, whom Jaguar's were testing, went to the left of him and crashed. I went to the right and ran over the legs of a photographer who was scrambling back through the hedge. I hit the hedge and skidded and hit the fence on the other side. I was burnt. But what was worrying me amid all the flames was that my Lotus had a magnesium body. It was the first magnesium-bodied car that Colin Chapman had built, and he and I were the only people who knew. If that magnesium had caught fire . . . There were and are many cars which used magnesium castings, but this was a whole aerodynamic body. It was one of Chapman's trade secrets. I was lucky. The car didn't catch fire. I went and tried to get Bill Smith out of his car, but he was dead. And the last I saw of the trim figure of Lance Macklin was him striding away in his trim overalls and with his helmet under his arm. As far as I know, he never raced again.'

Back to Lance Macklin. 'What had happened was that Mayers' Cooper-Climax tried to overtake the baulking Mercedes with one wheel on the grass on the downhill section just past the Deer's Leap. There was a milestone on the side of the road which he couldn't see. The front of Mayer's car hit this and, of couse, it just went up in the air, end over end and everybody piled into it. The result was that Mayers and Bill Smith were killed and Ken Wharton was badly burned.

'The Mercedes driver didn't even know what was happening. He just went gaily on. I went up to the organiser and said, "You should black-flag that man." And they did. They stopped him.

'This was far worse than Le Mans for me personally. To start with, I saw it coming. I had a good, or rather a bad, half-minute, I suppose, when I saw it happening, and I knew I couldn't do anything about it. I was going far too fast and it was downhill. It was the first time driving in motor races that I thought as I went into the pile-up: Death! I was convinced that I wouldn't be getting out of it.'

There was yet another victim of the Tourist Trophy before the race ended. R. L. Mainwaring's Elva had crashed . . . and he had been burned to death.

Peter Jopp is mistaken about one thing. The Tourist Trophy was not Lance Macklin's last race. Macklin says: 'After Dundrod I drove at Sebring with Archie Scott-Brown, a fabulous driver and a delightful man. I drove one more race after that, and by then it was summer and I hadn't got a drive in Formula One – John Heath had decided to pull out of Formula One racing. And then I was offered a job with Facel Vega, the French car firm.

'All my family were beginning to get upset, because I'd been involved in some nasty accidents, and they were pressing me to give up motor racing. I must admit that it was starting to lose some of its glamour for me. I'd been in it for eight or nine years, and after that time one misses having been reasonably settled. You travel so much in motor racing. You are forever in a plane or boat or train or driving somewhere. You are always living in a hotel. You are always having problems catching up with your laundry, getting your suits cleaned or your overalls washed. I don't suppose they have all those troubles nowadays, perhaps there's someone who does it all for them, but in those days it was quite tricky.'

*   *   *

155

Lance Macklin took the Facel Vega job, left motor racing behind him at the age of 35 and – somewhat reluctantly, he says – married and tried to settle down. 'Everything went well for the first year or two. I was working in Paris, and we bought a charming little house just outside the city. Facel gave me a very good expense account. My job was concerned with public relations, and they liked me to be seen around the best places, the ritzy restaurants. with my Facel Vega car parked outside. For a man living that sort of life in Paris the temptations, the sexual temptations, are very great. Paris is very well organised from a man's point of view. That is perhaps because the French have a different attitude to marriage. Many French marriages are still arranged, with the girl coming from a reasonably well-off family and bringing to the marriage enough money to pay for the upkeep of the home.

'When the couple have had a couple of children the husband will usually take a mistress, and, equally, the wife has a lover somewhere, with whom she jumps into bed.

'I found being married quite a different thing from living with someone for a month or two and then changing over to someone else. It was very different, being stuck to the same person month in, month out. Very constricting. And my wife, Sheila, was not a French girl, and when she sometimes caught me out it created problems.'

At Facel, Macklin teamed up with François Jardell. The Frenchman had been a member of a racing team called Los Amigos. But after the disaster he never drove a racing car again. And neither he nor Lance Macklin have ever gone back to Le Mans.

The Facel Vega failed to find enough buyers. The firm ran into difficulties, and so did the Macklin marriage. They came back to England . . . and divorce. Macklin coped with the problems of two young children, a boy and a girl, which meant a succession of nurses, nannies and *au pairs*.

At a party he met 'this nice little girl from New Zealand'. Eventually they married and went to live in New Zealand. It didn't last. He will cheerfully admit that he is not an ideal husband, while maintaining that there are few ideal wives.

Today he deals in property in Spain. He spends his summers skippering his beautiful little boat on charter round the

156

Mediterranean, a slim, elegant man with many memories and no regrets.

Motor racing? Ah, well, it isn't the same these days. The most he ever earned from it was around £5,000 a year, out of which he had to pay some expenses. But he and his friends on the tracks had fun. 'I don't think it's like that now,' he says.

What good came of it all?

The Le Mans disaster revealed that the safety measures there and on many other circuits throughout the world had become inadequate, almost futile, in the face of the ever-increasing advances in the performance of racing cars.

At Le Mans, the organisers, L'Automobile Club de l'Ouest, borrowed huge sums from the town and began a giant programme to make the circuit safer. The pits were moved back, increasing the distance between them and the spectators. A 'deceleration zone' or pit lane was constructed, earth banks were raised, and, perhaps most important, each of the sixty pits was given a new refuelling device to prevent the possibility of a crash causing a giant conflagration such as might very easily have happened in the 1955 race. The signalling was transferred via telephones from the pits to depots at the slowest part of the course, the Mulsanne corner. The Dunlop bend was lengthened and the bridge moved further on. An escape route was provided at Arnage, and the track was re-surfaced between White House and Tertre Rouge.

Fangio, speaking of safety measures at Le Mans, instanced the chicane introduced just before the pits. But this came years afterwards, in 1967. The Ferrari–Ford rivalry and the vogue of the big American engines gave rise to an astonishing increase in average speeds. The chicane brought these down past the pits and public enclosures. For a while. Technical progress sent them rising again.

At other tracks, too, organisers began to take stock, under pressure from their consciences, public opinion, and the insurance companies, in no particular order.

158

But safety in motor racing is a slow and expensive business, never catching up with the development of racing cars. Even today drivers will sometimes refuse to race in a Grand Prix because they consider the track inadequate and unduly dangerous.

In any case, motor racing *cannot* be made absolutely safe. Nor would it be right that it should be so, for the drivers at any rate. A completely safe motor race would be pointless. Racing is not like a game of cricket, tennis or football. Danger is built in to motor racing by its very nature. The skill and the catharsis, to be pretentious, lies in the brilliance of drivers in positions of danger, extricating themselves. This is the bond between the driver and the spectator. Driving on the edge of controllability, the limit, as they say, of man and machine, makes demands on the drivers and spectators alike. If a racing driver dies it is a common defeat. If he defeats death on the corners of the track, if he can control a sliding, spinning car, then this is a common victory.

As long as there is motor racing, it will be dangerous.

London, Paris, Stuttgart, 1975–6.

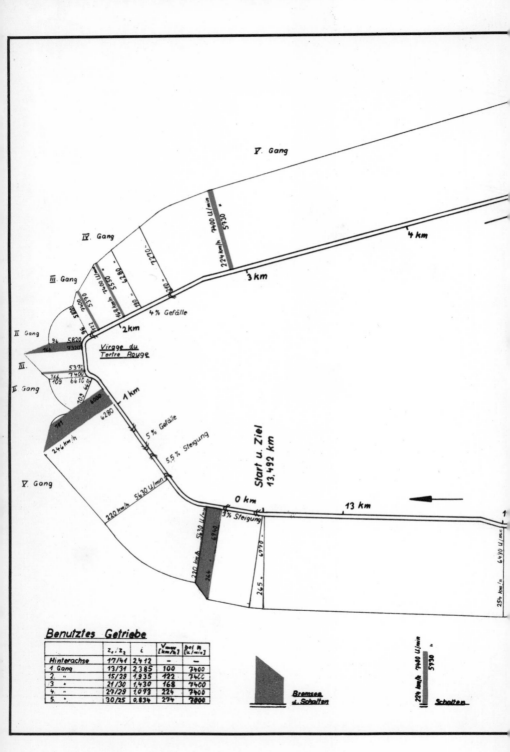

V. Gang

IV. Gang

7400 U/min

5730

224 km/h

4 km

3 km

III. Gang

7400 U/min

4280

5350

130

4% Gefälle

480 km/h

5370

5820

2400

2 km

II Gang

96 5820

166 7320

Virage du
Terte Rouge

III.

537%

744 7400

109 6610

II Gang

105

6000

1 km

6280

5% Gefälle

5,5% Steigung

181

244 km/h

V. Gang

220 km/h 5630 U/min

Start u. Ziel
13,492 km

0 km

3% Steigung

13 km

5630 U/min

6940

220 km/h

264

6970

265

6490 U/min

254 km/h

Benutztes Getriebe

	z_1/z_2	i	V$_{max}$ [km/h]	bei n [U/min]
Hinterachse	17/41	2,412	–	–
1 Gang	13/31	2,385	100	7400
2. "	15/29	1,935	122	7400
3. "	21/30	1,430	168	7400
4. "	27/29	1,073	224	7400
5. "	30/25	0,834	274	7000

Bremsen
u. Schalten

224 km/h 7400 U/min

5730

Schalten